Welcome to the Patchwork Zoo

Cat & Rabbit Door Decorations

Instructions on page 2.

ANIMAL PATCHWORK
CAT
RABBIT

Page 1 Cat & Rabbit Door Decorations

[Materials]

[Cat]

Red cotton fabric—35cm square
Red & white striped cotton fabric—20cm square
White cotton fabric—15cm square
Red chambray—15cm square
Quilt batting—25cm × 20cm
#25 Red embroidery floss

[Rabbit]

Blue cotton fabric—40cm × 35cm
Blue print on off-white fabric—20cm × 15cm
Off-white twill cotton fabric—20cm × 15cm
Blue & white cotton check fabric—20cm × 10cm
Quilt batting—25cm square
#25 Blue embroidery floss

[Directions]

1. Sew pieces together to make patchwork block.
2. Assemble patchwork block and quilt batting. Quilt as shown in illustration.
3. Embroider and appliqué pieces. With wrong sides together, assemble backing.
4. Fold backing edge over to patchwork block. Turn edges under and whipstitch all the way around so the block is bound by the backing.
5. Quilt all around binding.
6. Sew tapes on work for hanging.

[Drafting and Cutting]

Add 1 cm seam allowance and cut pieces.

Cat: Quilt batting—21cm × 17cm   Rabbit: Quilt batting—24cm × 21cm

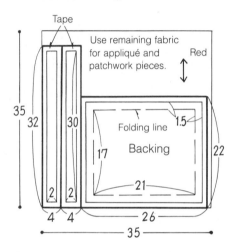

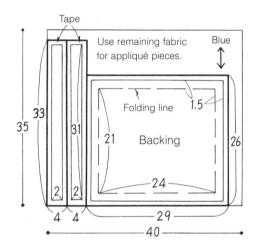

[Piecing]

Add 0.7cm seam allowance and cut pieces.

Cat

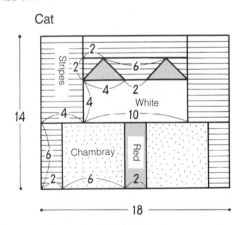

Rabbit

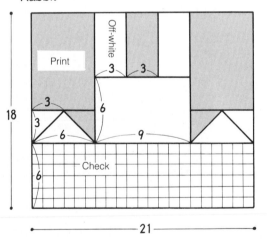

[Piecing Diagram]

Cat

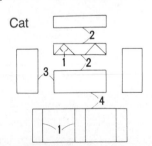

Rabbit

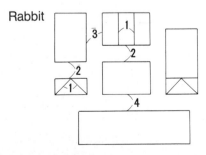

Cat

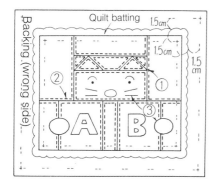

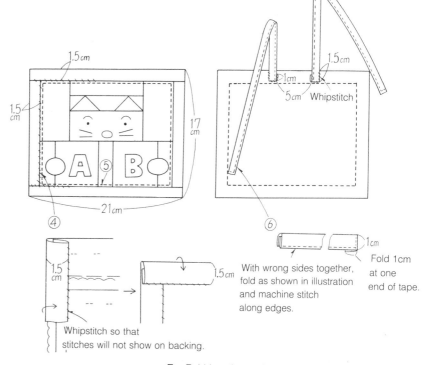

Quilt batting

Backing (wrong side)

1.5 cm
1.5 cm
1.5 cm

② ① ③

A B

1.5 cm

1.5 cm
cm

17 cm

④

21 cm

⑤

1cm
5cm Whipstitch

1.5cm

⑥

Fold 1cm at one end of tape.

1cm

1.5 cm

Whipstitch so that stitches will not show on backing.

1.5cm

With wrong sides together, fold as shown in illustration and machine stitch along edges.

For Rabbit, refer to directions on assembling Cat.

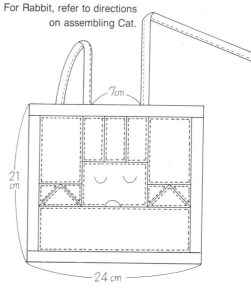

7cm

21 cm

24 cm

[Appliqué and Embroidery Pattern] (Actual size)

Add 0.5cm seam allowance and cut pieces. Sew on using blind stitch.
Use 3 strands of embroidery floss.

Cat

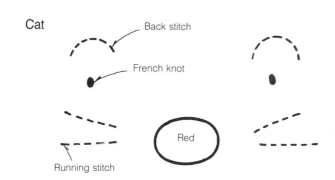

Back stitch

French knot

Running stitch

Red

Rabbit

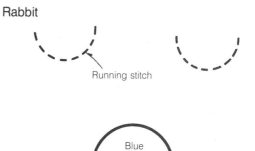

Running stitch

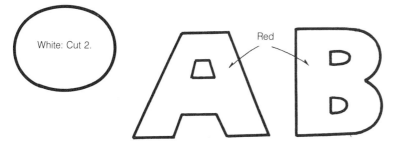

White: Cut 2.

Red

A B

Blue

3

Fun Tote Bags
and Backpacks

Eagle and Giraffe Bags

Instructions on page 6.

Pages 4 & 5 Eagle and Giraffe Bags

[Drafting and Cutting]

[Materials]

[Eagle]

Light blue print cotton fabric—90cm × 35cm
Brown print cotton fabric—60cm square
11 kinds of cotton fabric for patchwork piece
(Refer to photo.)
Cotton backing fabric—90cm × 35cm
Quilt batting—90cm × 35cm
#25 Black embroidery floss
4 Buttons (2cm in diameter)

[Giraffe]

Navy and white cotton fabric—90cm × 35cm
Beige print cotton fabric—60cm square
5 kinds of cotton fabric for patchwork piece
(Refer to photo.)
Cotton backing fabric—90cm × 35cm
Quilt batting—90cm × 35cm
#25 Embroidery floss in mustard, dark
yellow, brown, black
4 Buttons (2cm in diameter)

[Directions]

1. Sew pieces together to make patchwork blocks. (Iron seams towards animal motif so that animal block will show up.)
2. Embroider and appliqué pieces.
3. Sew border A and B to patchwork block.
4. Sew border C to (3).
5. Assemble patchwork block, batting and backing. Quilt in the ditch around all patchwork pieces. Quilt according to illustration on P. 67.
6. Quilt border pieces.
7. Assemble back, quilt batting and backing. Quilt according to illustration.
8. With right sides together, sew front and back. Finish seam edges.
9. Bind opening edge using 75cm bias strip (Refer to P. 69).
10. Make handles and attach with buttons.

Add seam allowance indicated in Parenthesis and cut pieces.
Cut batting in the following measurements: 2 pieces. 38cm × 32cm, 2 pieces 4cm × 31cm.

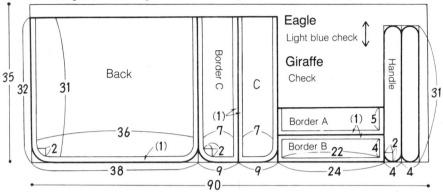

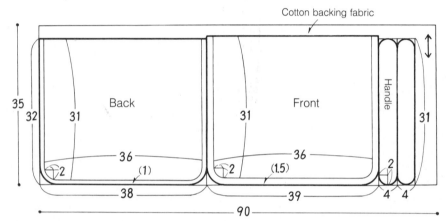

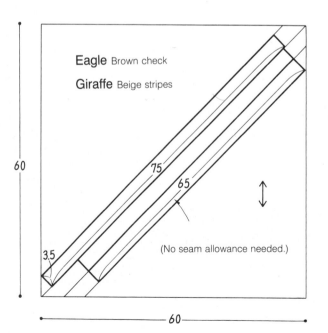

[Piecing]

Add 0.7cm seam allowance and cut pieces.

Eagle

Giraffe

[Piecing Diagram]

For assembling Eagle,
refer to Giraffe directions.

For (5), refer to illustration on P. 67.

Eagle

Giraffe

Border A

Border C

Border C

Border B

Batting

Backing

1.5cm 1.5cm

0.5 cm

Back

Backing

Batting

1.5cm

b. Use 65cm bias strip to bind edge.

0.9cm 1.2cm

a. Quilt.

Batting   Backing

c. Sew on buttons.

7cm   0.9cm

31cm

36cm

Continued on P. 67 for further illustrations.

a. Sew with right sides together.

Front   Back

b.

Bind seam and whipstitch in place.

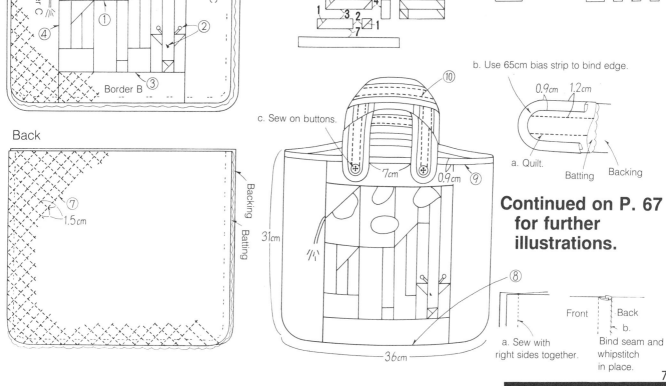

ANIMAL PATCHWORK
CAT

Cats —Bag, Lunch Bag, Shoe Bag—

Instructions on page 10.

Pages 8 & 9 Cats —Bag, Lunch Bag, Shoe Bag—

[Materials]

Blue cotton fabric—90cm × 100cm
Cream-colored cotton fabric—90cm × 95cm
White otton fabric—50cm square
Heavyweight quilt batting—90cm × 85cm
 # 25 Blue embroidery floss
2 Blue cotton cords (0.3cm in diameter, 70cm long)

[Directions]

[Bag]

1. Sew pieces together for patchwork blocks.
2. Sew borders A to patchwork blocks.
3. Sew borders B, C, D to (2).
4. Assemble front and batting. Quilt as shown in illustration.
5. Embroider and appliqué pieces.
6. Assemble back and batting. Machine stitch 0.2cm outside of finished line.
7. With right sides together, sew front and back. Turn inside out.
8. With right sides together, fold lining at fold line. Sew both side seams and turn inside out.
9. Make handles.
10. With wrong sides together, assemble (7) and (8). Insert handles and sew top edge.

[Drafting and Cutting] Add 1cm seam allowance and cut pieces.

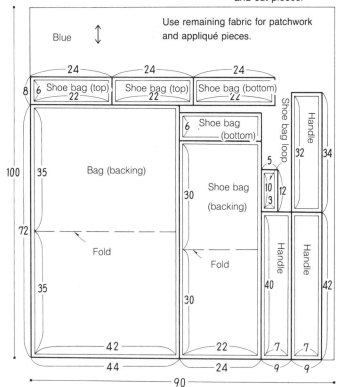

[Appliqué and Embroidery Pattern] (Actual size)

Add 0.3cm seam allowance and cut pieces. Sew on with blindstitch.

Use 3 strands of embroidery floss.

[Piecing]

Add 0.7cm seam allowance and cut pieces.

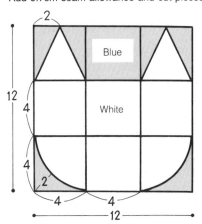

[Piecing Diagram]

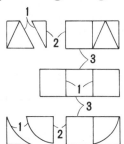

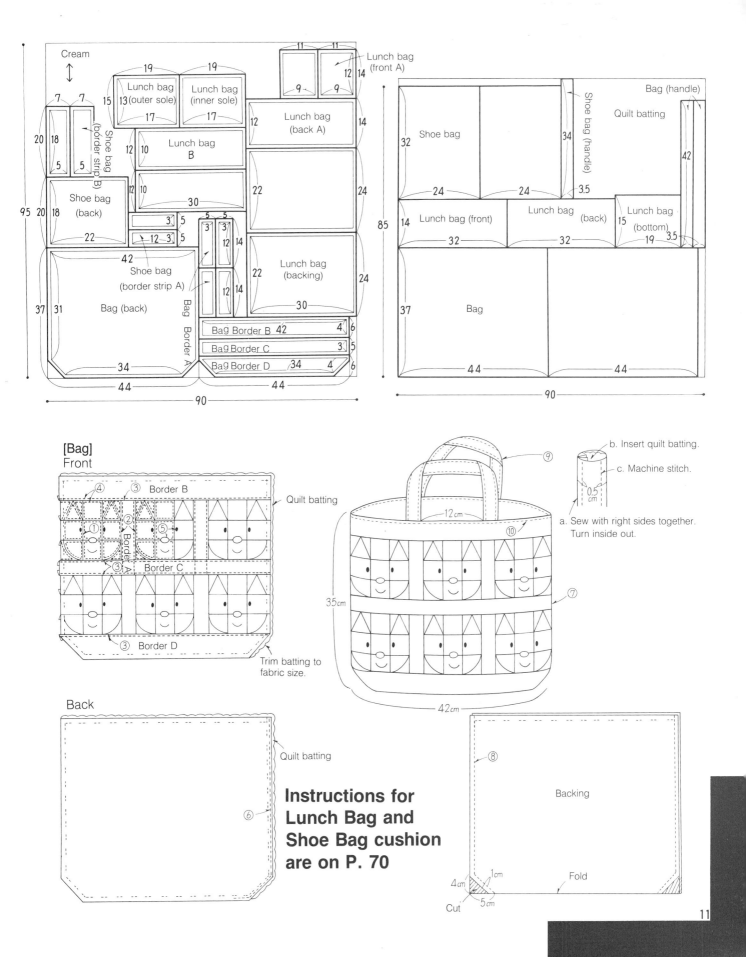

Cream

7 7
20 18
5 5

15 13 Lunch bag (outer sole) Lunch bag (inner sole)
19 19
17 17

Shoe bag (border strip B)

11 11
9 9
12 14 Lunch bag (front A)

Lunch bag (back A)
12 14

12 10 Lunch bag B

12 10

22 24

Shoe bag (back)
20 18

95

22

Bag Border A

42

Shoe bag (border strip A)

3 5
12 3 5

5 5
3 3
12 14
3 3
12 14
12 14

Lunch bag (backing)
22 24

30

37 31 Bag (back)

34

44 44

90

Bag Border B 42 4 6
Bag Border C 3 5
Bag Border D 34 4 6

Bag (handle)

Shoe bag
32 34
Shoe bag (handle)

Quilt batting
42

24 24 3.5

85

14 Lunch bag (front) Lunch bag (back) 15 Lunch bag (bottom) 3.5
32 32 19

37 Bag

44 44

90

[Bag]
Front

Border B
④ ③
② ① ⑤
③ Border C
Quilt batting

③ Border D

Trim batting to fabric size.

⑨
b. Insert quilt batting.
c. Machine stitch.
0.5 cm
a. Sew with right sides together. Turn inside out.

12cm
⑩
35cm
⑦
42cm

Back
Quilt batting
⑥

Instructions for Lunch Bag and Shoe Bag cushion are on P. 70

⑧
Backing

1cm
4cm
Cut
5cm
Fold

11

ANIMAL PATCHWORK
WHALE CHICK KANGAROO

Whale, Chick, Kangaroo —Drawstring Bags

Instructions for Whale Bag cushion are on P. 68.

Instructions for Chick and Kangaroo Bag cushion are on P. 14

Page 13 Chick & kangaroo Drawstring Bags

[Materials]

[Chick]

Green gingham fabric—40cm square
Off-white shirting fabric—20cm square
Mustard color shirting fabric—15cm square
Quilt batting—35cm × 20cm
#25 Dark brown embroidery floss
2 Yellow soft cotton cord (0.3cm in diameter, 50cm long)
Scotch tape

[Kangaroo]

Blue cotton fabric—60cm × 70cm
Light brown cotton fabric—25cm square
Brown cotton fabric—15cm × 10cm
Beige flowered print fabric—10cm square
Brown check cotton fabric—15cm square
Brown gingham scraps
Quilt batting—55cm × 35cm
#25 Dark brown embroidery floss
2 Blue soft cotton cords (0.5cm in diameter, 75cm long)
Scotch tape

[Drafting and Cutting]

Add 1cm seam allowance and cut pieces.
[Chick]: Cut 2 quilt battings
　　　　 in the measurements of 17cm × 19cm

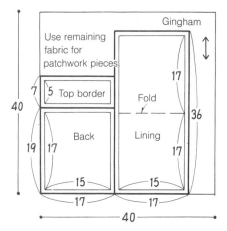

[Piecing] Add 0.7cm seam allowance and cut pieces.

Chick

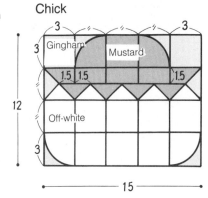

Kangaroo

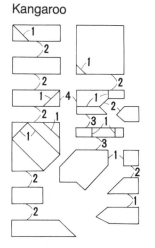

[Kangaroo]: Cut 2 quilt battings in the measurements of 26cm × 35cm

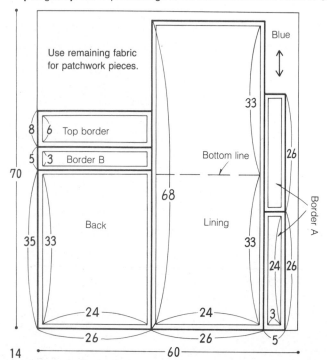

[Piecing Diagram]

Chick

Kangaroo

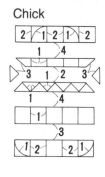

14

[Directions]
[Chick]

1. Sew pieces together for patchwork block.
2. With right sides together, sew top strip to patchwork block.
3. Assemble patchwork block and quilt batting. Quilt as shown in illustration.
4. Embroider and appliqué pieces.
5. Assemble back and quilt batting. Quilt 3cm wide horizontal lines.
6. With right sides together, sew front and back, leaving an opening for cords. Sew opening as shown in illustration.
7. With right sides together, sew lining as shown in illustration. Leave opening for turning bag inside out. Sew opening.
8. With right sides together, sew bag and lining at top edge Turn inside out at opening of lining and stitch the opening.
9. To make cord casement, machine stitch around top edge.
10. Insert cords and tie.

[Kangaroo]

Piece the patchwork block and sew borders A and B. Attach top strip. Refer to directions for [Chick] and proceed.

[Finished size]

[Chick] 15cm × 17cm
[Kangaroo] 24cm × 33cm

[Appliqué and Embroidery Patterns] (Actual size)

Add 0.5cm seam allowance and cut pieces. Sew appliqué pieces with blindstitch. Use 2 strands of embroidery floss.

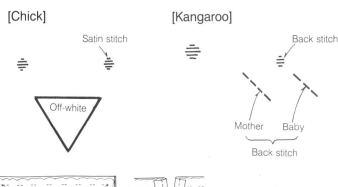

[Chick]   Satin stitch   Off-white

[Kangaroo]   Back stitch   Mother   Baby   Back stitch

[Chick]

Front

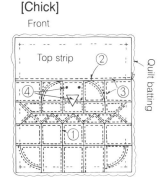

Top strip · ② · Quilt batting · ④ · ③ · ①

Back

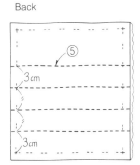

⑤ · 3cm · 3cm

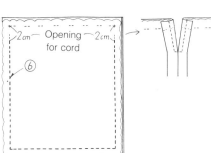

2cm — Opening for cord — 2cm · ⑥

2cm — Opening — 2cm for cord · Lining ⑦ · 8cm Opening for turning · Bottom

⑧

[Kangaroo]

Front

Top strip · Border A · Border A · Border B

Back

6cm · 6cm

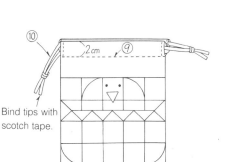

⑩ · 2cm · ⑨ · Bind tips with scotch tape.

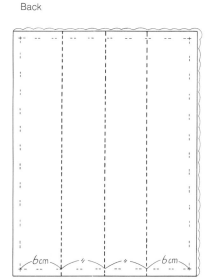

Lion Bags

Instructions on page 18.

P. 16 & 17 Lion Bags

[Materials]

[Materials needed for both bags]
(Yardage for 1 bag)

Cotton fabric for lining—
90cm × 55cm
Cotton backing fabric—
70cm × 50cm
Dark brown synthetic leather or
felt scraps
Quilt batting—70cm × 50cm
Linen facing—21cm square
2 Black buttons (0.7cm in
diameter)

[Girl Lion]

Blue-gray check cotton fabric: (small
check) 85cm × 30cm
(large check) 50cm × 25cm
Off-white cotton fabric—25cm × 20cm
Dark beige polka dot & flower print
fabric—20cm square
Pink check cotton fabric—15cm square
Off-white & dark brown plaid cotton
fabric scraps
Brown check cotton fabric scraps
#25 Brown embroidery floss
7cm White tulle lace (1.5cm wide)
20cm Pink satin ribbon (1cm wide)
1 Pearl bead (0.5cm in diameter)

[Boy Lion]

Blue-gray check cotton fabric: (large
check) 85cm × 30cm
(small check) 50cm × 25cm
Off-white cotton fabric—20cm square
Dark beige polka dot & flower print
fabric—20cm square
Navy blue, brown and white plaid cotton
fabric—15cm square
Brown print fabric 15cm × 10cm
Off-white & dark brown plaid cotton
fabric scraps
Brown check cotton fabric scraps
Black cotton fabric scraps
#25 Dark brown, moss green embroidery
floss

[Drafting and Cutting]

Add 1cm seam allowance and cut pieces.
Cut backing—2 backings (35cm × 25.5cm each) and 1 circle (23cm in diameter).
Cut quilt batting—2 each of the following: (35cm × 25.5cm) & (2.5cm × 23cm), 1 circle (23cm in diameter).
Cut linen facing: 1 circle (21cm in diameter)

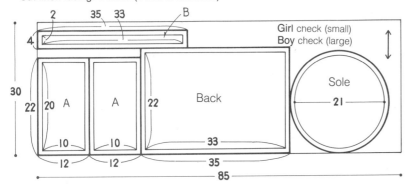

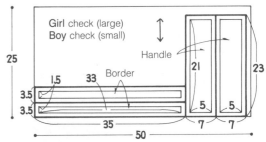

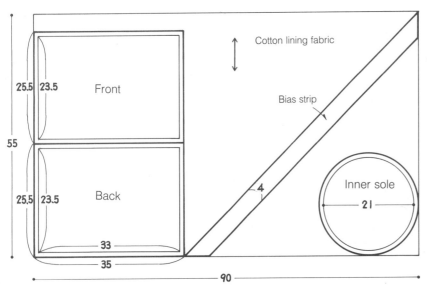

[Appliqué & Embroidery Patterns] (Actual size)

Cut all pieces except nose, adding 0.5cm seam allowance, and attach these appliqué pieces with blindstitch.

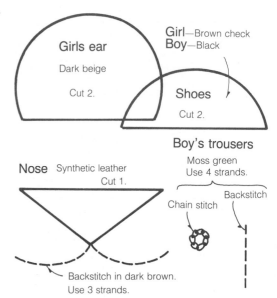

[Directions]

1. Sew pieces together for patchwork block. (Iron seam allowances towards animal motif so that animal piece will show up.)
2. Apply appliqué pieces and embroider.
3. Sew patchwork block and A.
4. Sew (3) and B.
5. Sew border and (4).
6. Assemble patchwork block, quilt batting and backing. Quilt as shown in illustration.
7. Sew buttons on.
8. Attach lace with whipstitch. Fold ribbon and attach pearl bead.
9. Sew back and border together. Assemble back, quilt batting and backing. Quilt as shown in illustration.

[Piecing]

Add 0.7cm seam allowance and cut pieces.

Girl
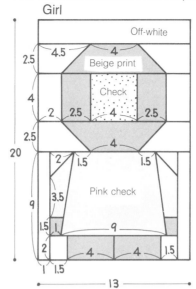

Boy
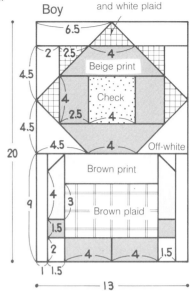

Navy blue, brown and white plaid

[Piecing Diagram]

Girl
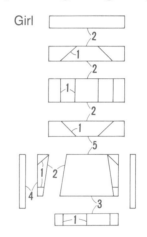

Boy
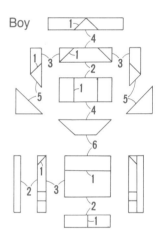

Front
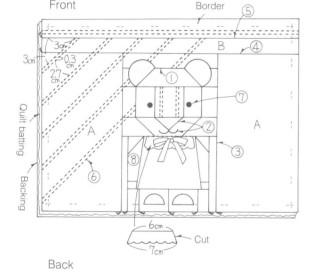

Back
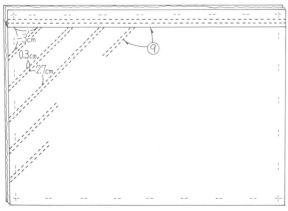

Refer to sewing diagram of [Girl] for [Boy].
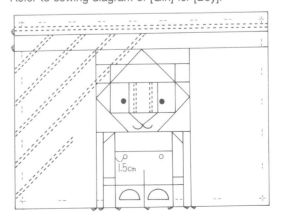

Continued on P. 83.

RABBIT TERRIER

Rabbit and Terrier Bags

Instructions on page 22.

P. 20 & 21 Rabbit and Terrier Bags

[Materials]
[Rabbit]

Red and off-white plaid cotton
fabric—90cm × 60cm
White flowers on gray cotton print
fabric—40cm × 30cm
Pink print on off-white fabric—30cm
square
Cotton backing fabric—80cm × 35cm
Quilt batting—90cm × 45cm
#25 Red embroidery floss
2 Shell buttons (1.9cm in diameter)

[Terrier]

Green and off-white plaid cotton
fabric—90cm × 60cm
Pink flower print on cream cotton
fabric—40cm × 30cm
Off-white broadcloth—30cm × 20cm
Brown and green check cotton
fabric—20cm square
Cotton backing fabric—80cm × 35cm
Quilt batting—90cm × 45cm
#25 Brown embroidery floss
2 Shell buttons (1.9cm in diameter)

[Directions]

1. Sew pieces together for patchwork
   block. (Iron seam allowances
   towards animal motif so that animal
   piece will show up.)
2. Embroider and appliqué pieces.
3. Center patchwork block on quilt
   batting cut to 45cm × 40cm. Quilt
   around the edges of animal motif.
   Quilt in the ditch in places as shown
   in illustration.
4. Sew backing and border B together.
5. Place border A, right sides together,
   and sew through quilt batting.

[Piecing] Add 0.7cm seam allowance and cut pieces.

Rabbit

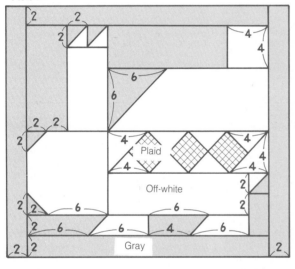

Terrier

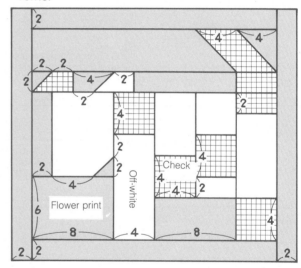

[Piecing Diagram]

Rabbit

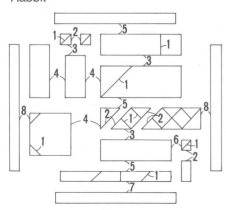

Terrier

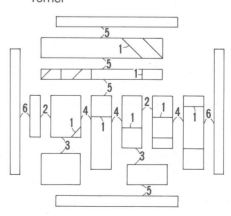

[Drafting and Cutting]

Add seam allowance indicated in parenthesis and cut pieces.
You will need 2 each of quilt batting: 45cm × 40cm, 3cm × 42cm.
Cut 2 pieces of backing: 40cm × 34cm each.

6. Sew borders B and C in the same manner as in (5).
7. Cut off the excess quilt batting at top and machine stitch.
8. Sew back and lining together.
9. Assemble quilt batting (45cm × 40cm) between back and lining and machine stitch as shown in illustration.
10. Assemble front and back. Trim back to fit the size of front. Bind edges with bias strip. (Refer to P. 69.)
11. Make handles and attach.
12. Sew buttons on front.

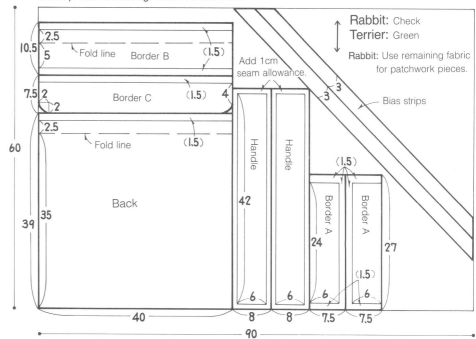

Rabbit: Check
Terrier: Green

Rabbit: Use remaining fabric for patchwork pieces.

Add 1cm seam allowance.

Bias strips

Border B — Fold line — 2.5 / 5 / 10.5 / (1.5)
Border C — 7.5 / 2 / 2 / (1.5) / 4
Back — Fold line — 2.5 / (1.5) / 60 / 39 / 35
Handle — 42 / 6 / 8
Handle — 6 / 8
Border A — 24 / 6 / 7.5 / (1.5) / 3
Border A — 27 / 6 / 7.5 / (1.5) / 3
40 — 90

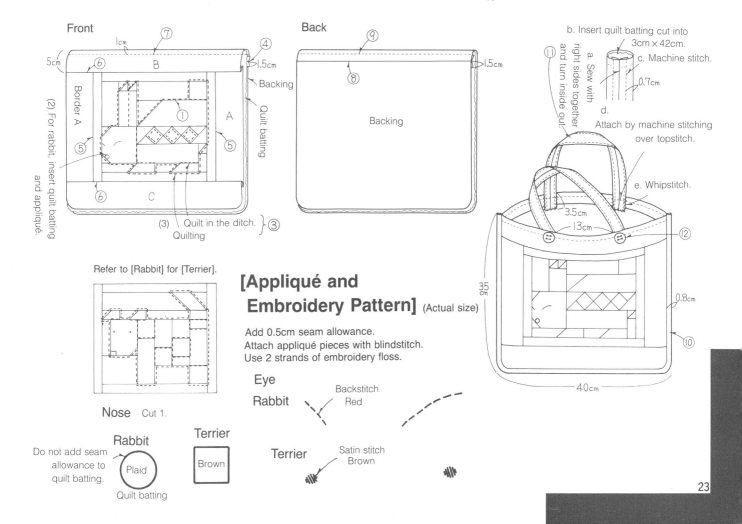

Front
1cm ⑦
5cm ⑥
B ④ 1.5cm
Backing
Border A ① A
⑤ ⑤
Quilt batting
(2) For rabbit, insert quilt batting and applique.
⑥ C
(3) Quilt in the ditch. ③
Quilting

Back
⑨
⑧ 1.5cm
Backing

b. Insert quilt batting cut into 3cm × 42cm.
a. Sew with right sides together and turn inside out.
⑪
c. Machine stitch.
0.7cm
d. Attach by machine stitching over topstitch.
e. Whipstitch.
3.5cm
13cm
⑫
35cm
0.8cm
⑩
40cm

Refer to [Rabbit] for [Terrier].

Nose   Cut 1.

[Appliqué and Embroidery Pattern] (Actual size)

Add 0.5cm seam allowance.
Attach appliqué pieces with blindstitch.
Use 2 strands of embroidery floss.

Eye
Rabbit   Backstitch Red

Terrier   Satin stitch Brown

Rabbit
Plaid
Quilt batting
Do not add seam allowance to quilt batting.

Terrier
Brown

ANIMAL PATCHWORK
HARE
ELEPHANT

Hare and Elephant Backpack

Instructions on page 26.

ANIMAL PATCHWORK
MONSTER

Monster Bag with Pencil Case

Instructions on page 72.

P. 24 Hare and Elephant Backpack

[Materials]
[Hare]

Off-white print fabric—50cm × 40cm
Pink print fabric—75cm × 25cm
Dark brown cotton fabric—20cm × 10cm
Light brown cotton fabric—15cm square
Cotton backing fabric—80cm × 45cm
Quilt batting—90cm × 55cm
#25 Dark brown, pink, brown embroidery floss
1 zipper (50cm long)
2 Dark brown cotton tape (2.5cm wide, 25cm long)
2 Dark brown cotton tape (2.5cm wide, 14cm long)
1 Dark brown cotton tape (2.5cm wide, 20cm long)
4 Dark brown plastic "D" rings (2.5cm wide)
Polyester stuffing

[Elephant]

Beige cotton fabric—50cm × 40cm
Navy print fabric—75cm × 25cm
Navy plaid cotton fabric—20cm square
Royalblue, light blue cotton fabric—each 15cm × 10cm
Cotton backing fabric—80cm × 45cm
Quilt batting—90cm × 55cm
#25 Pink, white embroidery floss
1 zipper (50cm long)
2 Navy cotton tape (2.5cm wide, 25cm long)
2 Navy cotton tape (2.5cm wide, 14cm long)
1 Navy cotton tape (2.5cm wide, 20cm long)
4 Navy plastic "D" rings (2.5cm wide)

[Drafting and Cutting] Add seam allowance indicated in parenthesis and cut pieces.

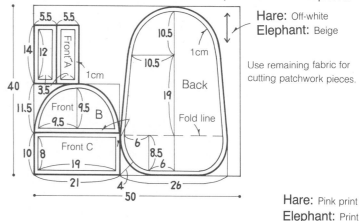

Hare: Off-white
Elephant: Beige

Use remaining fabric for cutting patchwork pieces.

Hare: Pink print
Elephant: Print

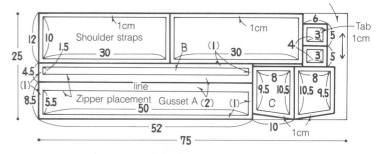

Size of quilt batting is shown in shaded areas. Add 1cm seam allowance and cut. You will need 2 each of the following besides the previously mentioned pieces: 12cm × 28cm, 2cm × 5cm.

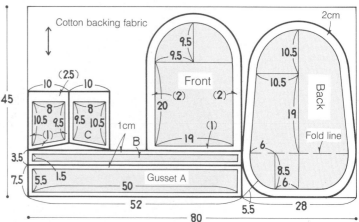

[Embroidery Pattern] (Actual size)

Hare

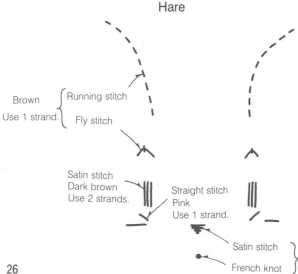

Brown Use 1 strand. { Running stitch / Fly stitch }

Satin stitch Dark brown Use 2 strands.

Straight stitch Pink Use 1 strand.

Satin stitch } Pink Use 2 strands.
French knot }

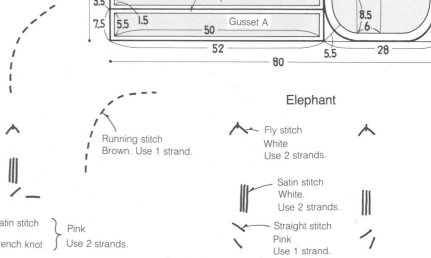

Running stitch Brown. Use 1 strand.

Elephant

Fly stitch White Use 2 strands.

Satin stitch White. Use 2 strands.

Straight stitch Pink Use 1 strand.

[Directions]

1. Sew pieces together to make patchwork block.
2. Sew A, B, C to patchwork block.
3. Embroider.
4. Assemble patchwork block, batting and backing. Quilt as shown in illustration.
5. Attach tail.
6. Assemble back, batting and backing. Quilt on fold line and 3cm wide lines as shown in illustration.
7. Assemble gusset, batting and backing. Quilt gusset A and C.
8. Finish off edge and apply zipper.
9. Sew tabs.
10. With right sides together, sew gusset A, B to gusset C, inserting tabs. Finish off edges.
11. Sew shoulder straps.
12. Assemble shoulder straps and cotton tape, baste to back.
13. Sew on tape for "D" rings.
14. With right sides together, sew front, gusset and back. Finish off edges.

[Piecing] Add 0.7cm seam allowance and cut pieces.

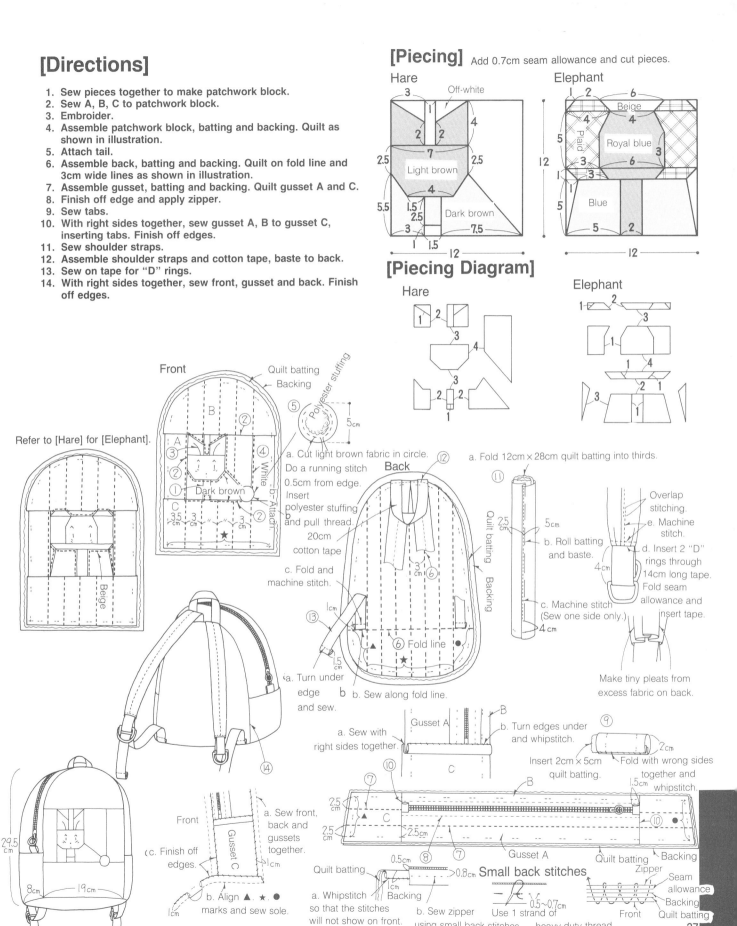

Hare
3
Off-white
1
4
2 2
7
2.5 Light brown 2.5
4
5.5 1.5
2.5
3 Dark brown 7.5
1 1.5
12
12

Elephant
1 2 6
Beige
4 4
5 Plaid Royal blue 3
3 6
1 3
1
5 Blue
5 2
12

[Piecing Diagram]

Hare
1 2
3
4
3
2 2
1

Elephant
1 2
3
1 4
1
2 1
3 1

Refer to [Hare] for [Elephant].

Front
Quilt batting
Backing
Polyester stuffing
B
A
3
2
1 Dark brown
C
3.5cm 3cm 3cm
White
b. Attach
5cm
a. Cut light brown fabric in circle. Do a running stitch 0.5cm from edge. Insert polyester stuffing and pull thread.
20cm cotton tape
c. Fold and machine stitch.

Beige

Back
12
3cm
6
1cm
13
1.5cm
a. Turn under edge and sew.
b. Sew along fold line.
6 Fold line

a. Fold 12cm × 28cm quilt batting into thirds.
11
2.5cm 5cm
4cm
b. Roll batting and baste.
c. Machine stitch (Sew one side only.)
4cm

Overlap stitching.
e. Machine stitch.
d. Insert 2 "D" rings through 14cm long tape. Fold seam allowance and insert tape.
Make tiny pleats from excess fabric on back.

Gusset A
B
a. Sew with right sides together.
b. Turn edges under and whipstitch.
10
C
Insert 2cm × 5cm quilt batting.
9
2cm
Fold with wrong sides together and whipstitch.
1.5cm

29.5cm
8cm 19cm

Front
Gusset C
a. Sew front, back and gussets together.
c. Finish off edges.
1cm
b. Align ▲ ★ ● marks and sew sole.
1cm

7
2.5cm
2.5cm
C
▲
2.5cm
8
7
Gusset A
Quilt batting
0.5cm
a. Whipstitch Backing so that the stitches will not show on front.
b. Sew zipper using small back stitches.
>0.8cm Small back stitches
0.5~0.7cm
Use 1 strand of heavy-duty thread.
B
10
Quilt batting
Zipper
Seam allowance
Backing
Front Quilt batting

27

ANIMAL PATCHWORK
BUTTERFLY

Butterfly Bag and Pouch

Instructions on page 30.

P. 28 & 29 Butterfly Bag and Pouch

[Materials]

Cream-colored flower print fabric—90cm × 70cm
White flower print fabric—40cm square
Mustard cotton fabric—40cm square
Green cotton fabric scraps
Cotton backing fabric—90cm × 60cm

2 Off-white bias strips (for handle) (2.5cm wide, 55cm long)
Quilt batting—90cm × 60cm
Cardboard—25cm square
#25 Dark brown embroidery floss
2 White tulle lace (4.5cm wide, 20cm long)

1 Off-white tulle lace (1cm wide, 80cm long)
1 Off-white tulle lace (1cm wide, 26cm long)
2 Mustard color ribbon (0.3cm wide, 15cm long)
2 Off-white cotton tape (0.6cm wide × 30cm long)
2 Gold cords (0.3cm in diameter, 90cm long)
22 Round glass beads (medium size)
4 Decorative clasps (1cm wide, 1cm in diameter)
1 set magnet snaps (1.3cm in diameter)
Polyester stuffing

[Drafting and Cutting]

Add seam allowance indicated in parenthesis and cut pieces.

Cut 2 each from quilt batting in following sizes
41cm × 30cm   25cm × 26.5cm   54cm × 3cm

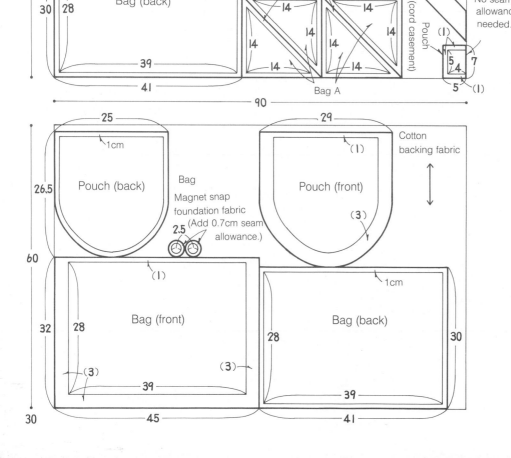

Bag decoration

White flower print

0.5cm

3 3

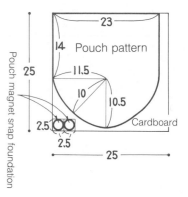

Pouch pattern

Pouch magnet snap foundation

23
14
25
11.5
10
10.5
2.5
2.5
25
Cardboard

[Directions]
[Bag]

1. Sew pieces together for patchwork block.
2. Embroider.
3. Sew patchwork block and A.
4. Sew B with (3).
5. Assemble patchwork block, quilt batting and backing. Quilt in the ditch.
6. Assemble back, quilt batting and backing. Quilt as shown in illustration.

[Piecing] Add 0.7cm seam allowance and cut pieces.

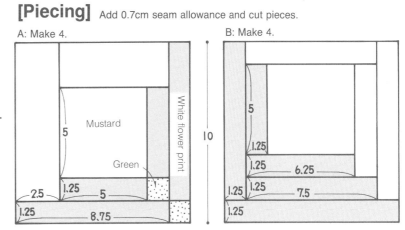

A: Make 4.

Mustard
Green
White flower print
5
2.5
1.25
5
1.25
8.75
10
10

B: Make 4.

5
1.25
1.25
6.25
1.25
1.25
7.5
1.25
10
10

[Piecing Diagram]

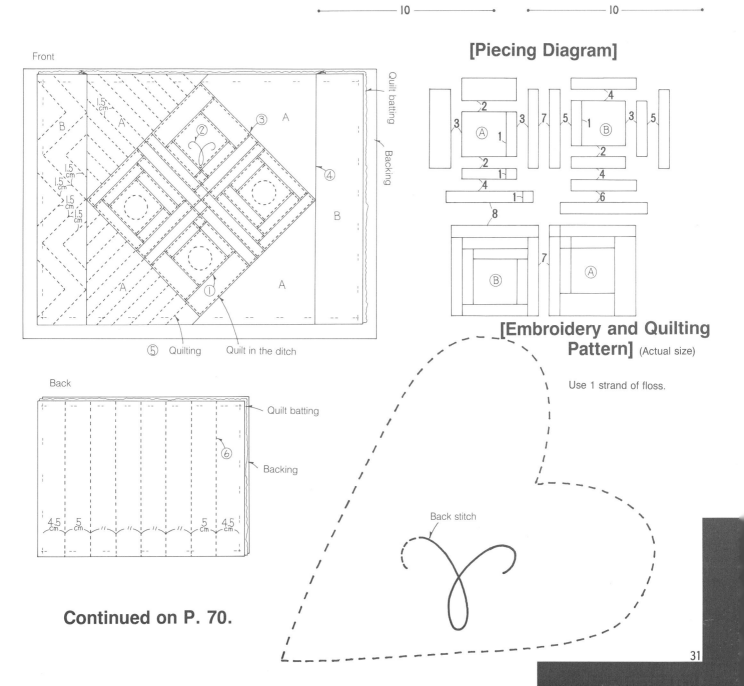

Front

Quilt batting

Backing

1.5 cm
1.5 cm
1.5 cm
1.5 cm
1.5 cm

B
A
A
②
③
A
④
B
A
①

⑤ Quilting   Quilt in the ditch

3 2 3 7 5 4 1 3 5
Ⓐ 1
2
1
4
1
8

4
Ⓑ 1
2
4
6

Ⓑ 7 Ⓐ

Back

Quilt batting

⑥

Backing

4.5 cm   5 cm   5 cm   4.5 cm

Continued on P. 70.

[Embroidery and Quilting Pattern] (Actual size)

Use 1 strand of floss.

Back stitch

31

and Playrooms

ANIMAL PATCHWORK
PENGUIN OWL HORSE

Penguin, Owl, Horse—Framed Pictures

Instructions on page 34.

P. 32 & 33 Penguin, Owl, Horse— Framed Pictures

[Materials]

[Materials needed for all three projects]

(Yardage for 1 project)

2 Quilt batting—20cm square
Cardboard—20cm square
White frame (Inside measurements are 18cm square.) (Inside measurements of photo frames are generally 18.7cm square.)
Scotch tape

[Penguin]

Black and white print fabric—30cm square
White cotton fabric—20cm × 15cm
White on black plaid cotton fabric—20cm × 15cm
White polka dots on red fabric—10cm square
#25 Black, pink embroidery floss

[Owl]

Brown gingham fabric—30cm × 25cm
Brown print on beige cotton fabric—20cm × 15cm
Dark brown cotton fabric—15cm square
Brown, off-white, crimson cotton scraps
#25 Black, white embroidery floss

[Piecing]

Add 0.7cm seam allowance and cut pieces unless indicated otherwise.

[Penguin]

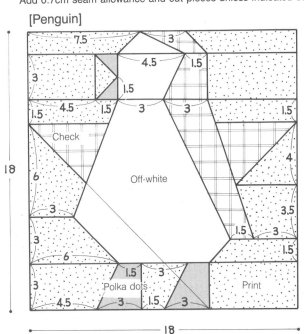

[Owl]

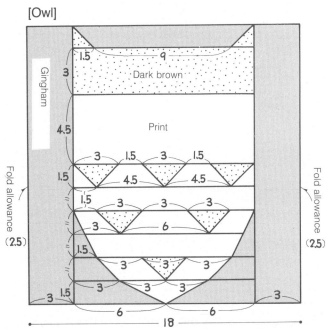

[Piecing Diagram]

Penguin

Owl

Rocking Horse

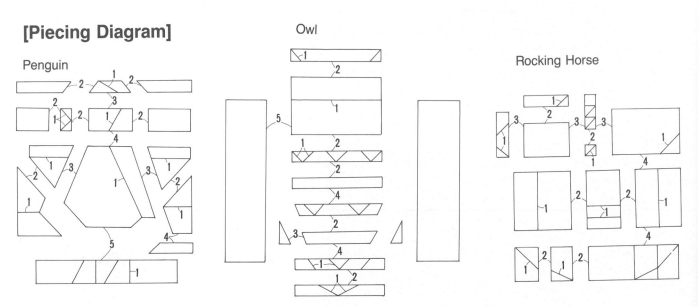

34

[Rocking Horse]

Green cotton fabric—30cm × 25cm
Heart print on off-white fabric—15cm × 20cm
Brown flower print—15cm square
Blue flower print—10cm square
Dark brown cotton scraps
#25 Black, pink, white embroidery floss

[Directions]

1. Sew pieces together for patchwork block.
2. Embroider. (For the [Owl], embroider and sew on appliqué.)
3. Assemble patchwork block and quilt batting. Quilt as shown in illustration.
4. Sew on strips to top and bottom of patchwork block. These strips will be folded to the back when framing.
5. Sew on strips to both sides as previously mentioned.
6. Assemble patchwork block, quilt batting and cardboard. Tape folded strips to back with scotch tape.

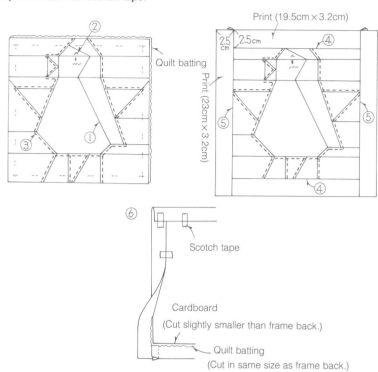

Refer to [Penguin] for [Owl] and [Rocking Horse].

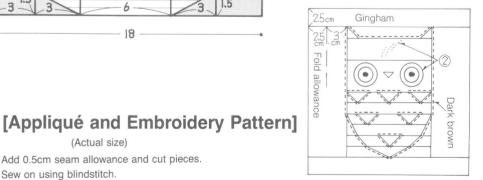

[Appliqué and Embroidery Pattern]

(Actual size)

Add 0.5cm seam allowance and cut pieces.
Sew on using blindstitch.

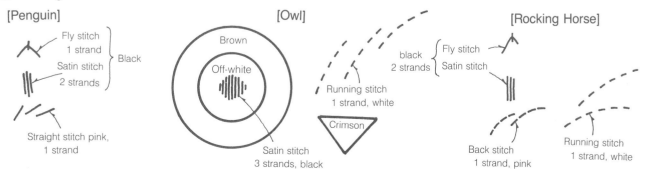

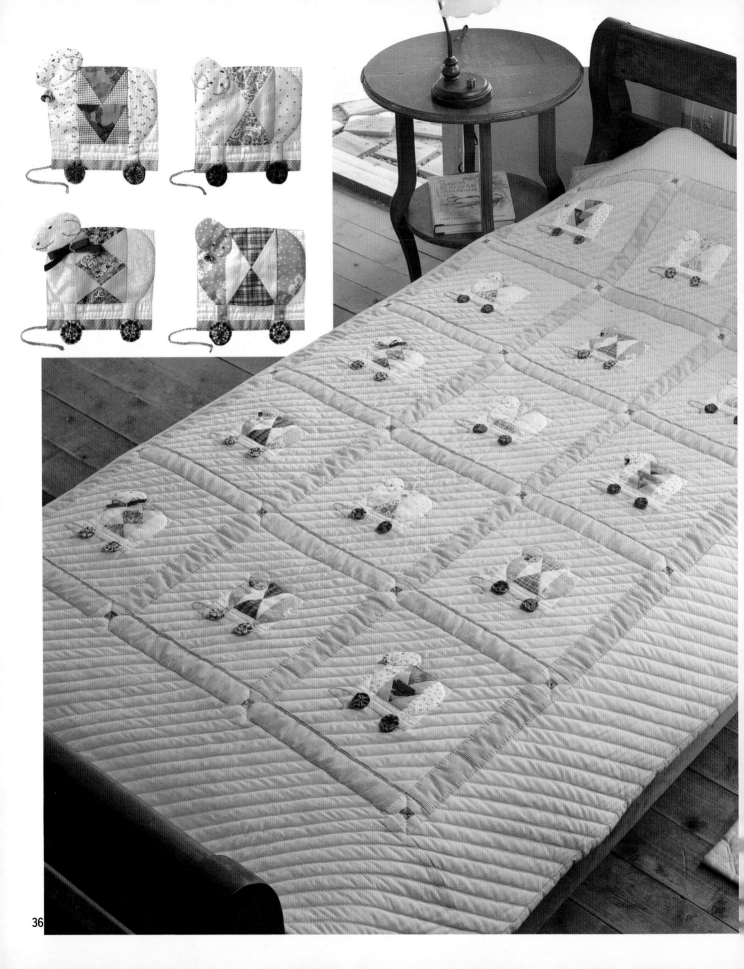

ANIMAL PATCHWORK
SHEEP

Sheep Bed Quilt and Mat

Instructions on page 38.

P. 36 & 37 Sheep—Bed Quilt and mat

[Drafting and Cutting]

Add 1cm seam allowance and cut pieces.
Cut quilt batting in the following measurements
96cm × 133cm (Cut 2.) and 69cm × 44cm (Cut 1).

[Materials]

Brown on white check cotton fabric—110cm × 400cm
Beige cotton fabric—90cm × 310cm
Off-white cotton fabric—90cm × 40cm
White polka dots on sand-beige fabric—50cm × 30cm
Light green cotton fabric—40cm square
Green flower print fabric—20cm square
Off-white, beige, etc. cotton scraps for patchwork block (Refer to photo.)
Quilt batting—100cm × 310cm
#25 Dark brown, sand-beige, beige, white embroidery floss
4 Purple grosgrain ribbons (0.6cm wide, 16cm long)
4 Gold bells (1cm in diameter)
3 Silver bells (1cm in diameter)

Use remaining fabric for patchwork pieces.

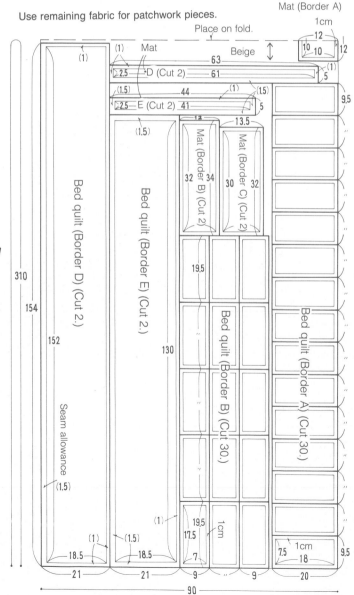

Place on fold.

Plaid

Fold line

1.5

25.5

1.5

1cm   1cm

Mat
backing

Cut 2.

74   69

Center

Fold line

Bed quilt (Backing) (Cut 2.)

400

1.5
22

27

197

192

Center

Bed quilt (Border C) (Cut 38)

1cm

27   25

4.5
6.5   6.5   70

66.5

1.5

Mat (Border A)
1cm
12
10   10   12
Place on fold.
Beige

(1)   Mat

(1)
63
2.5   D (Cut 2)   61
5
9.5
(1.5)   44   (1)   (1.5)
2.5   E (Cut 2)   41
5

(1.5)

12   13.5

Mat (Border B) (Cut 2)
32 34
Mat (Border C) (Cut 2)
30 32

Bed quilt (Border D) (Cut 2.)

Bed quilt (Border E) (Cut 2.)

310

154

152

130

19.5

Bed quilt (Border B) (Cut 30.)

1cm

Bed quilt (Border A) (Cut 30.)

Seam allowance

(1.5)

(1)

19.5
17.5
1cm
7

(1)   (1.5)

18.5   18.5

21   21

9   9

7.5   1cm
18
9.5

20

110

90

[Directions]
[Bed quilt]

1. Sew pieces together to make patchwork blocks.
2. Sew sheep blocks to borders A and B following steps (a) through (d).
3. Embroider and sew on appliqué pieces.
4. Sew small 9-patch block to border C lengthwise.
5. Sew sheep blocks to border C lengthwise.
6. Sew (4) and (5) together.
7. Sew border D to left and right side of quilt.
8. Sew border E to top and bottom of quilt.
9. With right sides together, sew center seam of backing.
10. Assemble quilt top, batting and backing. Quilt in the ditch in designated areas and quilt as shown in illustration.
11. Crease backing at fold line. Fold towards quilt top and finish edges.
12. Make wheels and attach to quilt.
13. Attach ribbons and bells.

Continued on P. 77.

[Piecing]
Add 0.7cm seam allowance and cut pieces.

Father sheep: Make 3 blocks.

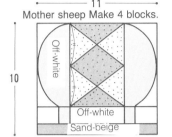

Boy Make 4 blocks. Girl Make 6 blocks

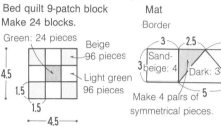

Mother sheep Make 4 blocks.

Bed quilt 9-patch block Make 24 blocks.

Green: 24 pieces
Beige 96 pieces
Light green 96 pieces

Mat
Border
Sand-beige: 4
Dark: 34
Light: 30
Make 4 pairs of symmetrical pieces.

Flag: Make 4.
Print Solid

[Piecing Diagram]

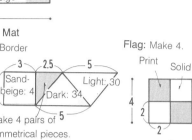

[Bed Quilt]

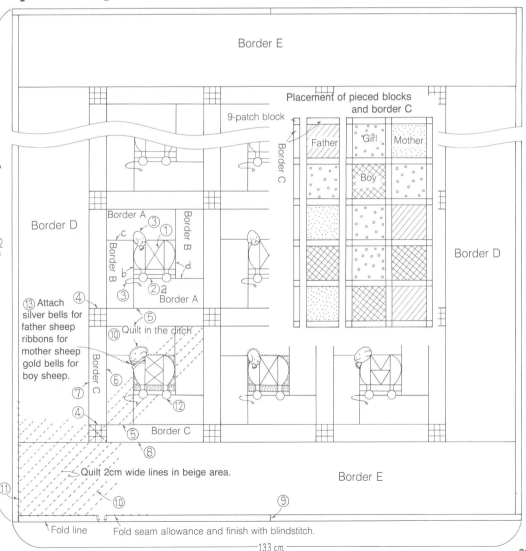

Border E

Placement of pieced blocks and border C

9-patch block

Border C

Father Girl Mother
Boy

Border D

Border D

Border A
Border B
Border B
Border A

Border C

⑬ Attach silver bells for father sheep ribbons for mother sheep gold bells for boy sheep.

⑩ Quilt in the ditch

Quilt 2cm wide lines in beige area.

Border C

Border E

192 cm

133 cm

Fold line
Fold seam allowance and finish with blindstitch.

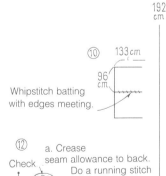

⑩ 133cm
96 cm
Whipstitch batting with edges meeting.

⑫
Check
5 cm
back
a. Crease seam allowance to back. Do a running stitch 0.2cm from edge.
0.7cm seam allowance

2.5 cm
b. Pull thread at both ends and make a neat circle. Tie ends.

39

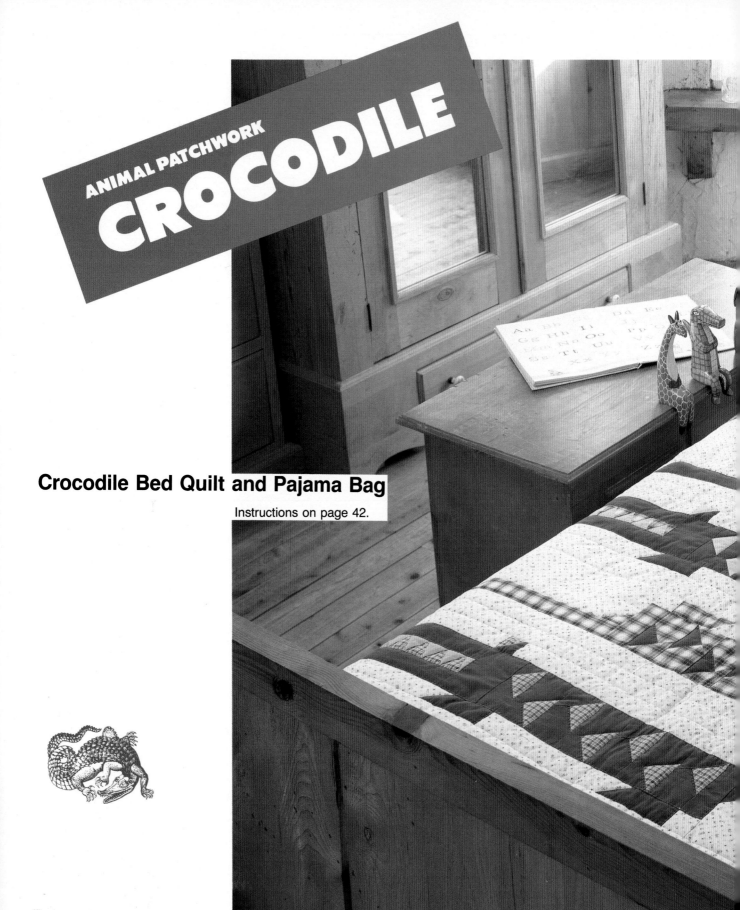

ANIMAL PATCHWORK CROCODILE

Crocodile Bed Quilt and Pajama Bag

Instructions on page 42.

40 & 41 Crocodile Bed Quilt and Pajama Bag

[Materials]

Off-white flower print fabric—90cm × 300cm
Dark brown cotton fabric—90cm × 200cm
Brown cotton fabric—90cm × 80cm
Brown gingham—90cm × 80cm
Red plaid cotton fabric—90cm × 60cm
Beige cotton fabric—70cm × 35cm
Bright yellow cotton fabric—70cm × 25cm
Green and off-white check cotton fabric—70cm × 25cm
Green plaid cotton fabric—45cm × 50cm
Cream-color flower print fabric—35cm square
Orange flower print fabric—35cm square
Light blue cotton fabric—35cm square
Moss green cotton fabric—25cm square
Red flower print fabric—25cm square
Blue plaid cotton fabric—25cm square
Cotton backing fabric—90cm × 410cm
Quilt batting—120cm × 380cm
2 Dark brown cords (0.7cm in diameter, 100cm long)

[Drafting and Cutting]
Add seam allowance indicated in parenthesis and cut pieces.

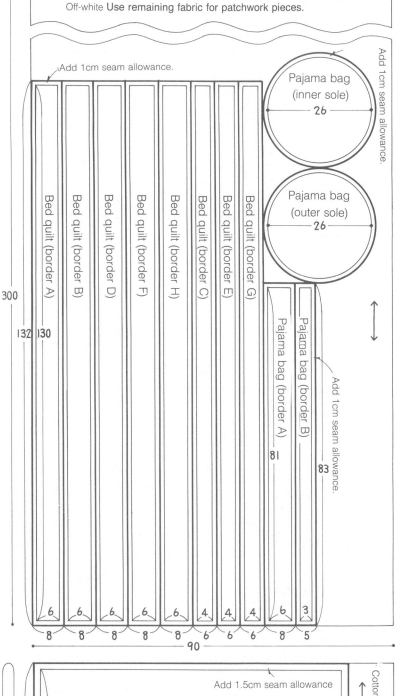

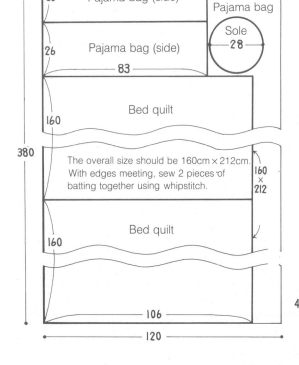

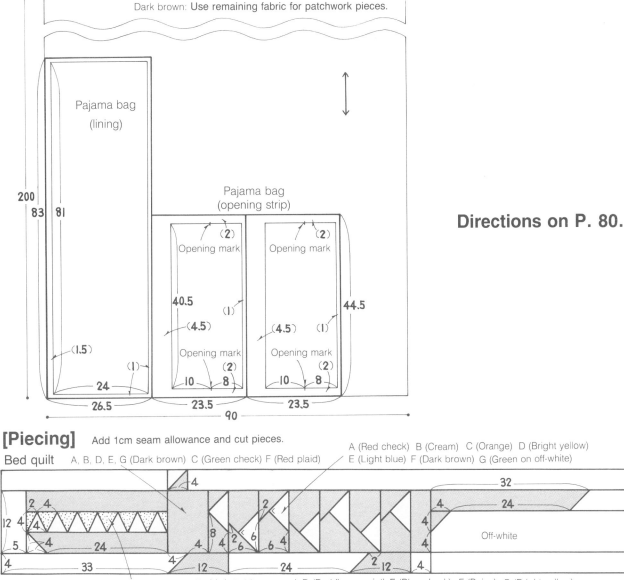

Dark brown: Use remaining fabric for patchwork pieces.

Pajama bag
(lining)

200
83 81

Pajama bag
(opening strip)

(2)
Opening mark

(2)
Opening mark

40.5

(1)

(4.5)

44.5

(4.5)   (1)

Opening mark
(2)

Opening mark
(2)

(1.5)

(1)

24
26.5

10   8
23.5

10   8
23.5

90

Directions on P. 80.

[Piecing]   Add 1cm seam allowance and cut pieces.

Bed quilt   A, B, D, E, G (Dark brown) C (Green check) F (Red plaid)

A (Red check) B (Cream) C (Orange) D (Bright yellow)
E (Light blue) F (Dark brown) G (Green on off-white)

20

4

2 4
12 4
4
5   4
4

8
4 2
6

2
6

6   4

32

4   24

4

4

Off-white

4

33

4

12

24

2 12

4

130

A (Beige) B (Green on off-white) C (Moss green) D (Red flower print) E (Blue check) F (Beige) G (Bright yellow)

Pajama bag   Dark brown   Red plaid

Beige

15

3 1.5 3

3

3

6 3

1.5
1.5

3

15

3

3

1.5

4.5

1.5

3

Off-white

3   18

3 3

3

18

2.5   9

3

3   21

9

4.5

81

Bed quilt border

Symmetrical triangles: 4 each

10   13   26

10   4 Brown

20 Gingham

26

[Piecing Diagram]   For pajama bag, refer to bed quilt.

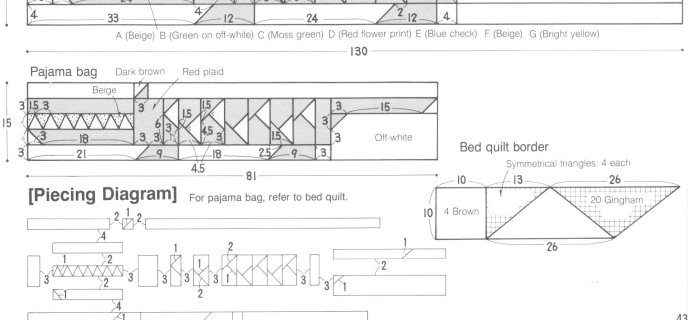

2 1 2
4

1   2
1   3
3 2
2
1

1   2
2

3   3 1 3

1
2

2

3 1 3

1

1
2

1
2

3 1

1

2

4

1

ELEPHANT RABBIT CAT DOG

Elephant, Rabbit, Cat Cushions
Dog Mini-cushion

Instructions for Elephant and Rabbit Cushions are on P. 46.
Instructions for Cat Cushions are on P. 74
and Dog Mini-cushion, on P. 76.

P. 44 & 45 Elephant and Rabbit Cushions

[Materials]

[Materials needed for both projects]

Cotton fabric for back—55cm × 50cm
Cotton backing fabric—50cm square
Quilt batting—50cm square
Zipper (39cm long)
Uncovered cusion—47cm square

[Elephant]

Beige print fabric—70cm × 50cm
Dark brown print fabric—30cm square
Gray print fabric—25cm square
Print scraps: Gray polka dots, Green, Black, Reddish-brown, Off-white
Brown print fabric scraps (Refer to photo.)
#25 Black embroidery floss

[Rabbit]

Blue-gray check fabric—60cm × 50cm
Gray print fabric—30cm × 25cm
Off-white print fabric—30cm × 20cm
Brown print fabric—30cm × 5cm
Beige print fabric—20cm × 10cm
Blue print scraps (Refer to photo.)
#25 Reddish-brown, Black embroidery floss

[Drafting and Cutting]

Cut backing and quilt batting in the size of 47cm square. You will need 1 of each.
Refer to [Elephant] for [Rabbit] ④(4) Refer to additional illustration.

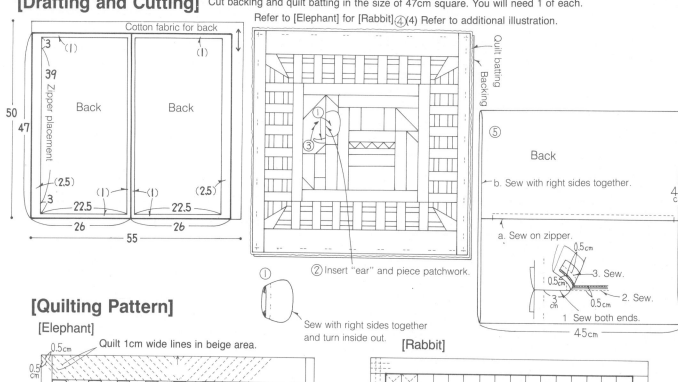

② Insert "ear" and piece patchwork.

① Sew with right sides together and turn inside out.

a. Sew on zipper.
b. Sew with right sides together.
1 Sew both ends.
2. Sew.
3. Sew.

[Quilting Pattern]

[Elephant]

Quilt 1cm wide lines in beige area.

Quilt in the ditch in the areas marked with bold lines.

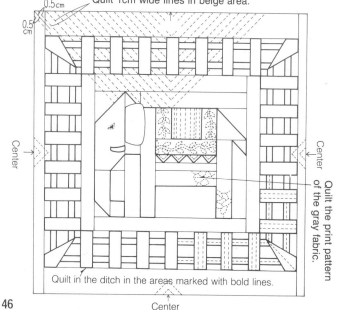

[Rabbit]

Quilt in the ditch in the areas marked with bold lines.

Quilt

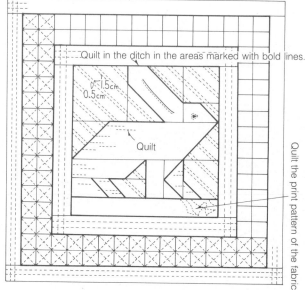

[Directions]

1. Make "ears." Appliqué "tusk."
2. Sew pieces together to make patchwork block.
3. Embroider.
4. Assemble patchwork block, quilt batting and backing. Quilt in the ditch and quilt as shown in illustration.
5. Sew and finish cushion.

[Pattern, Appliqué & Embroidery Patterns] (Actual size)

Add 0.7cm seam allowance to pattern and cut pieces. For appliqué pieces, add 0.3cm seam allowance. Appliqué using blindstitch.

[Elephant]

Eyes Use 2 strands.

Satin stitch   Outline stitch

Tusk

Off-white

Ears
Gray polka dots
Cut 2.

Opening

Place on fold.

[Rabbit]

Eyes

Outline stitch

Satin stitch

Ears

Outline stitch
Use 2 strands black embroidery floss.

Use 3 strands reddish-brown embroidery floss.

[Piecing]

[Elephant] Add 0.7cm seam allowance and cut pieces.

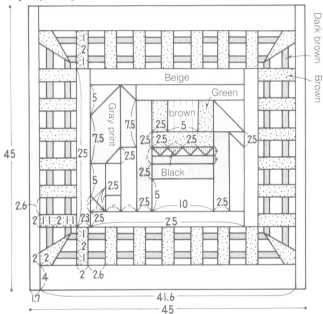

Dark brown   Brown

Beige

Green

brown

Gray print

Black

45

41.6

45

1.7

[Rabbit]

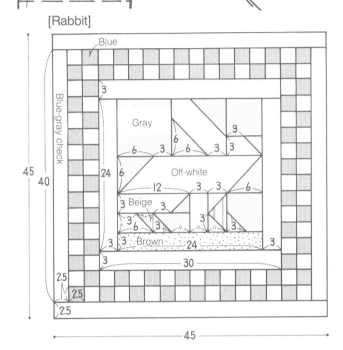

Blue

Blue-gray check

Gray

Off-white

Beige

Brown

45   40

30

45

[Piecing Diagram]

[Elephant]

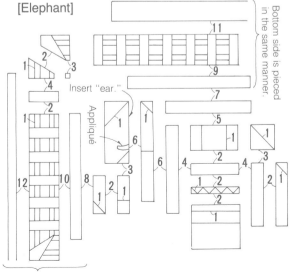

Insert "ear."

Appliqué

Bottom side is pieced in the same manner.

Right side is pieced in the same manner.

[Rabbit]

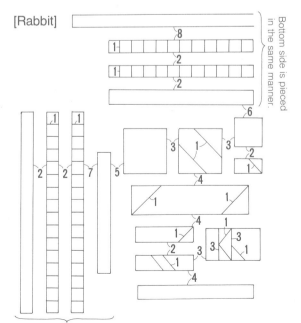

Bottom side is pieced in the same manner.

Right side is pieced in the same manner.

47

ANIMAL PATCHWORK
LION

Lion Wall Pockets

Instructions on page 50.

RABBIT CAT MONKEY ELEPHANT

Rabbit, Cat, Monkey, Elephant Wall Pocket

Instructions on page 78.

P. 48 Lion Wall Pocket

[Materials]

Blue cotton fabric—90cm × 110cm
Black cotton fabric—90cm × 50cm
Yellow cotton fabric—60cm × 20cm
Dark yellow cotton fabric—60cm × 20cm
Light brown cotton fabric—40cm × 30cm
Green cotton fabric—35cm × 40cm
Red cotton fabric—35cm × 20cm
Brown print fabric—30cm square
Brown & White gingham—20cm × 10cm
Cotton scraps: Off-white, White, Charcoal gray
Felt scraps: White, Black
Quilt batting (light weight)—60cm × 40cm
Quilt batting (medium weight)—50cm × 55cm
#25 Charcoal gray embroidery floss

[Directions]

1. Sew pieces together to make lion's face.
   Piece lion's mane and feet. (Iron seam allowance towards motif so that the design will show up.)
2. Blindstitch (1) to fabric used for pockets.
3. Embroider and attach appliqué pieces.
4. With right sides together, sew pockets and gussets.
5. Layer with lightweight quilt batting (59cm × 18cm) and backing fabric for pockets. Quilt in the ditch using black thread.
6. Bind top edge of pockets with 59cm bias strip. (Refer to P. 69 for binding directions.)
7. For pockets A, B, C, fold gussets and baste. Bind with 47cm bias strip.
8. Assemble foundation and medium weight quilt batting. Quilt as shown in illustration with black thread.

[Drafting and Cutting]

Add seam allowance indicated in parenthesis and cut pieces.
Cut 2 lightweight quilt batting 59cm × 18cm.
Cut medium weight quilt batting 47cm × 54cm.

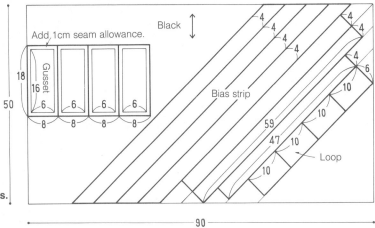

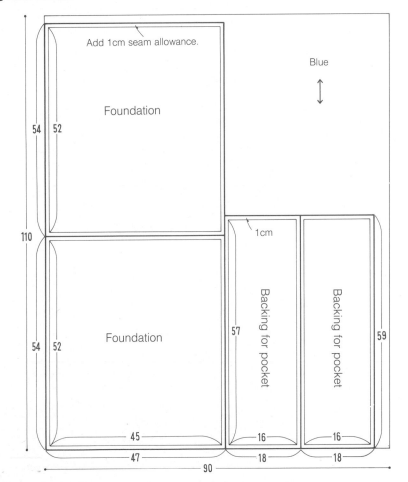

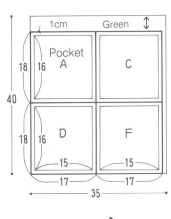

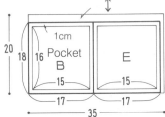

9. Affix pockets to foundation and sew through center of gusset.
10. Sew along edge of bias strip at bottom of pockets A, B, C.
11. Apply bias strip around edge of foundation.
12. Make four loops of black cotton and attach to foundation.

[Patchwork Pattern] (Actual size)

Add 0.7cm seam allowance and cut pieces.

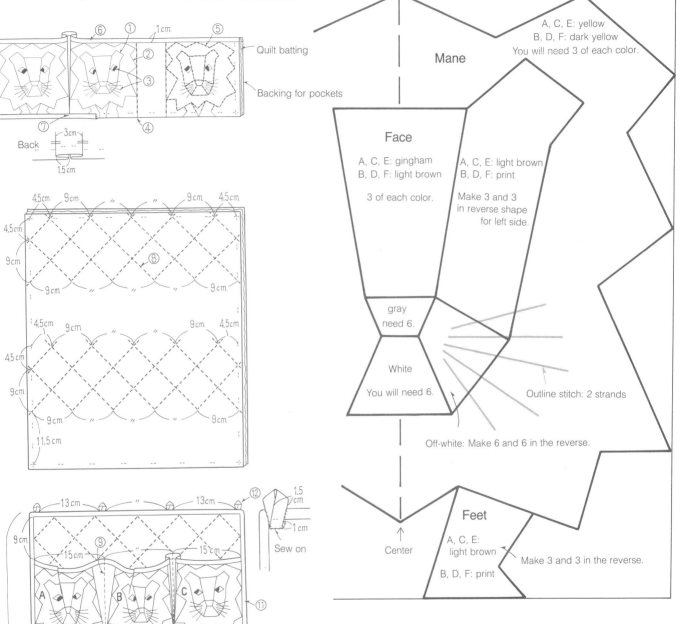

Mane

A, C, E: yellow
B, D, F: dark yellow
You will need 3 of each color.

Face

A, C, E: gingham
B, D, F: light brown

3 of each color.

A, C, E: light brown
B, D, F: print

Make 3 and 3
in reverse shape
for left side.

gray
need 6.

White
You will need 6.

Outline stitch: 2 strands

Off-white: Make 6 and 6 in the reverse.

Center

Feet

A, C, E:
light brown

B, D, F: print

Make 3 and 3 in the reverse.

Dark brown

Quilt batting

Backing for pockets

Back

3cm

1.5cm

1cm

Sew on

1.5cm

1cm

Eyes for A, F (Actual size)
(Refer to eyes A, F for eyes B- E and appliqué using blindstitch.)

(No seam allowance needed.)

White felt

Black felt
(Affix on black felt.)

51

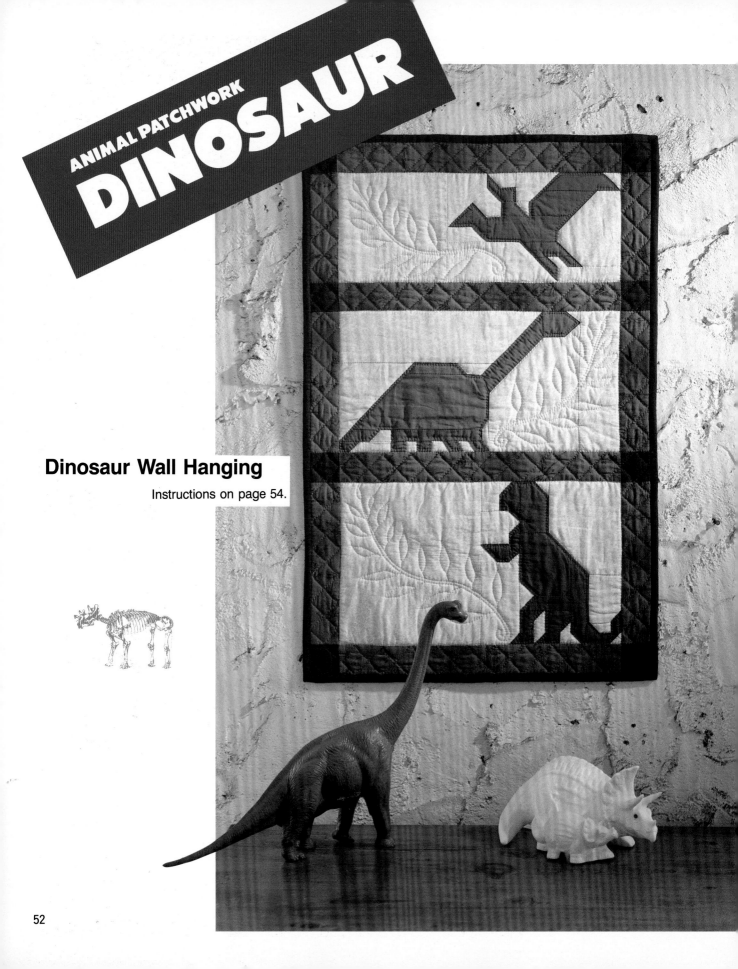

ANIMAL PATCHWORK
DINOSAUR

Dinosaur Wall Hanging

Instructions on page 54.

Stuffed Terrier Toys

Instructions on page 81.

P. 52 Dinosaur Wall Hanging

[Materials]

Beige fabric—90cm × 40cm
Brown print fabric—90cm × 25cm
Dark brown cotton fabric—90cm × 20cm
30cm squares cotton fabric in Blue, Green, Brown
Cotton backing fabric—50cm × 80cm
Quilt batting—50cm × 80cm

[Drafting and Cutting]

Add seam allowance indicated in parenthesis and cut pieces.
Cut 1 each of backing and quilt batting in the following measurements: 49cm × 74cm.

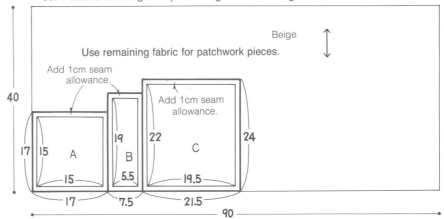

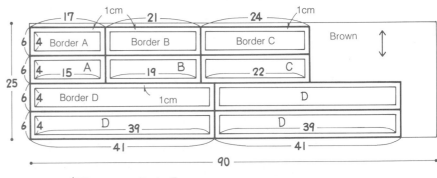

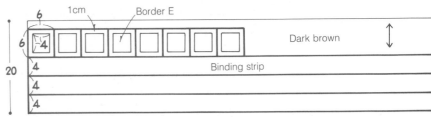

[Piecing Diagram]

Winged dinosaur

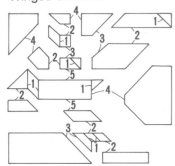

[Piecing]

Add 0.7cm seam allowance and cut pieces.

Winged dinosaur

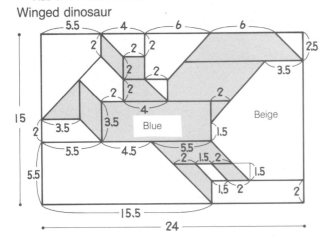

Tyrannosaurus

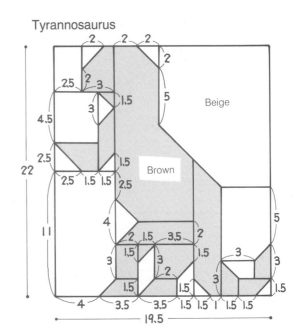

54

[Directions]

1. Sew pieces together to make patchwork blocks.
2. Sew A to winged dinosaur, B to Brontosaurus, C to Tyrannosaurus.
3. Sew borders A, B, C to (2).
4. Sew on borders D and E.
5. Sew (3) and (4).
6. Assemble patchwork top, quilt batting and backing. Quilt in the ditch and quilt as shown in illustration.
7. Bind edges with binding strips. (Refer to P. 69.)

Quilting patterns on page 84.

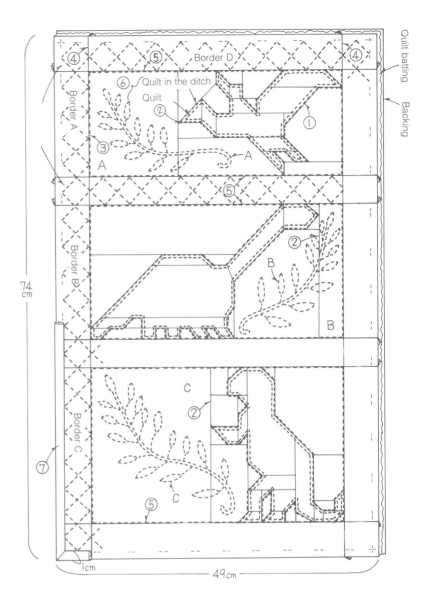

Tyrannosaurus

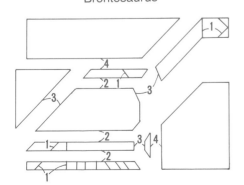

Brontosaurus

Brontosaurus

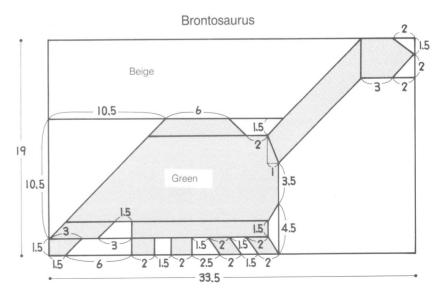

Stuffed Bears

Instructions on page 58.

P. 56 & 57 Stuffed Bears

[Materials]
[Large]

White cotton fabric—approximately 90cm × 130cm
Assorted print fabric in Reds, Pinks and Beige (Refer to photo.)
Cotton backing fabric—approximately 90cm × 165cm
Quilt batting—90cm × 165cm
Black felt scraps
#25 Black embroidery floss
2 Black semicircular buttons for eyes (1.5cm in diameter)
4 White buttons (1.5cm in diameter)
85cm Ribbon (2.5cm wide)
Polyester stuffing

[Small]

White cotton fabric—approximately 90cm × 70cm
Red print fabric scraps (Refer to photo.)
Cotton backing fabric—approximately 90cm × 85cm
Quilt batting—90cm × 85cm
Black felt scraps
#25 Black embroidery floss
2 Black semicircular buttons for eyes (1cm in diameter)
4 White buttons (1.2cm in diameter)
40cm Ribbon (1.5cm wide)
Polyester stuffing

[Directions]

1. Piece red and white or light and dark to make a checkerboard patchwork pattern.
2. Assemble patchwork pieces, quilt batting and backing. Quilt as shown in illustration.
3. Place patterns on quilted piece and cut out pieces.
4. Lay fabric for ears right sides together and place on batting. Sew around ears leaving an opening.
5. With right sides together, sew center seam of head and face.
6. Insert ears and with right sides together, sew head and face.
7. Turn inside out. Stuff firmly with polyester stuffing.
8. Sew center seam of body (back) and body (front).
9. With right sides together, sew back and front of body. Turn inside out and stuff firmly with polyester stuffing.
10. Sew arms as shown in illustration.
11. With right sides together, sew legs.
12. Turn legs inside out. Stuff firmly and whipstitch feet.
13. Sew head to body.
14. Attach arms and legs to body with white buttons.
15. Make face.
16. Tie ribbon.

[Piecing]

Add 0.7cm seam allowance and cut pieces.

Large
Red and White / light and dark
110 pieces each
Small
Red and White
55 pieces each

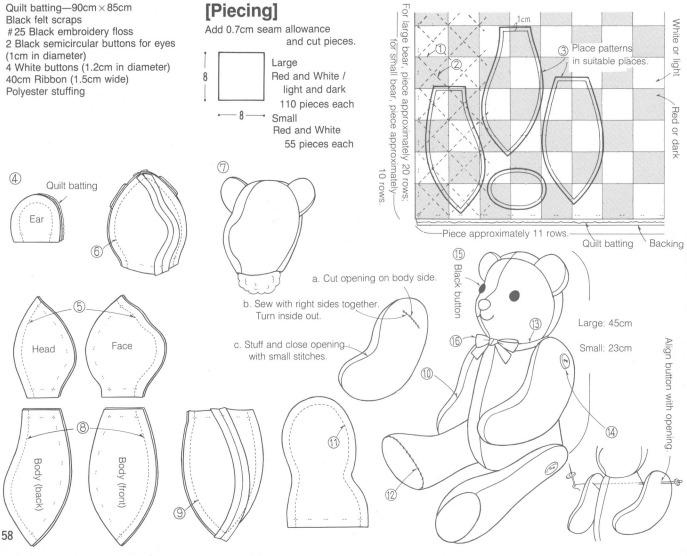

58

[Pattern for Small Bear] (Actual size)

Add 1cm seam allowance
and cut pieces.

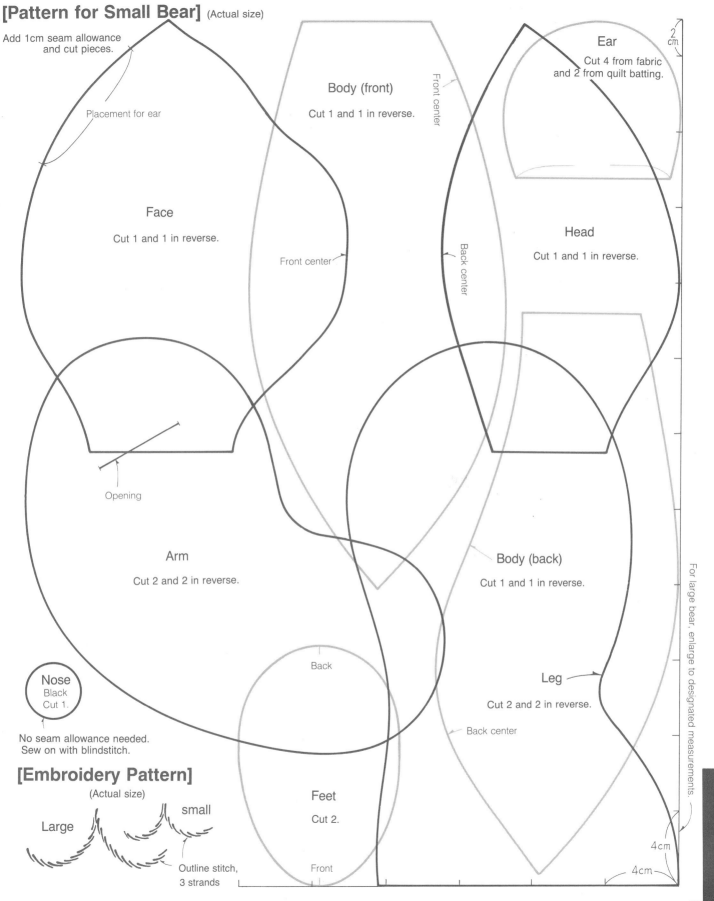

Placement for ear

Body (front)

Cut 1 and 1 in reverse.

Front center

Ear

Cut 4 from fabric
and 2 from quilt batting.

2 cm

Face

Cut 1 and 1 in reverse.

Front center

Back center

Head

Cut 1 and 1 in reverse.

Opening

Arm

Cut 2 and 2 in reverse.

Body (back)

Cut 1 and 1 in reverse.

Back

Nose
Black
Cut 1.

No seam allowance needed.
Sew on with blindstitch.

Leg

Cut 2 and 2 in reverse.

Back center

For large bear, enlarge to designated measurements.

[Embroidery Pattern]

(Actual size)

small

Large

Feet

Cut 2.

Front

Outline stitch,
3 strands

4cm

4cm

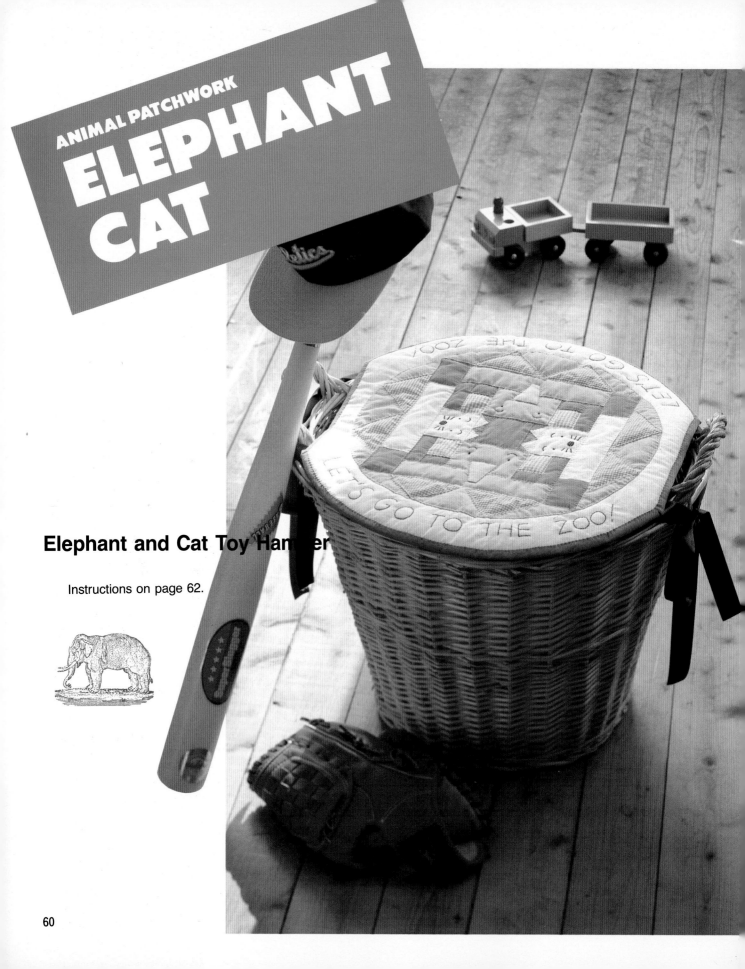

ANIMAL PATCHWORK
ELEPHANT
CAT

Elephant and Cat Toy Hamper

Instructions on page 62.

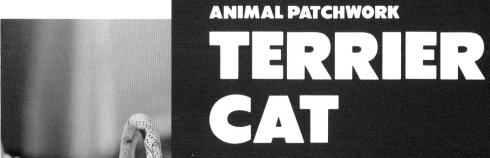

ANIMAL PATCHWORK

TERRIER CAT

Terrier and Cat Mini-bucket

Instructions on page 82.

P.60 Elephant and Cat Toy Hamper

[Materials]

Green cotton fabric—75cm × 50cm
White cotton fabric—60cm × 50cm
Green chambray—40cm × 30cm
Green gingham—35cm × 20cm
Blue cotton fabric—20cm square
Blue gingham scraps
Cream-color cotton fabric scraps
White polka dots on red fabric scraps
Quilt batting—50cm square
#25 Green, Blue, Red embroidery floss
Cardboard—50cm square
4 Green satin ribbons (2.5cm wide, 60cm long)

[Drafting and Cutting]

Add seam allowance indicated in parenthesis and cut pieces.
Cut 1 quilt batting in circle (46cm in diameter).
Cut cardboard in the same shape as backing but without seam allowance.

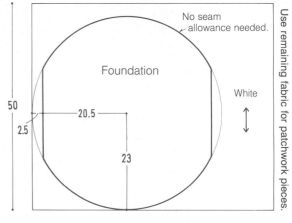

[Appliqué and Embroidery Patterns]

(Actual size)

Add 0.5cm seam allowance and cut pieces.
Attach appliqué using blindstitch.
Use 3 strands of embroidery floss.

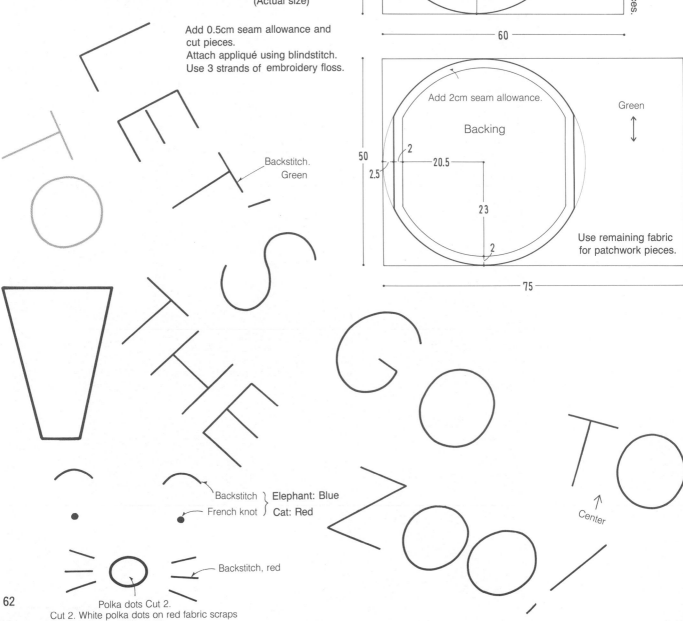

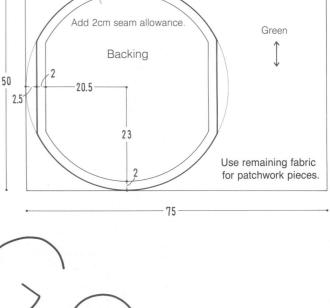

Backstitch. Green

Backstitch   } Elephant: Blue
French knot } Cat: Red

Backstitch, red

Polka dots Cut 2.
Cut 2. White polka dots on red fabric scraps

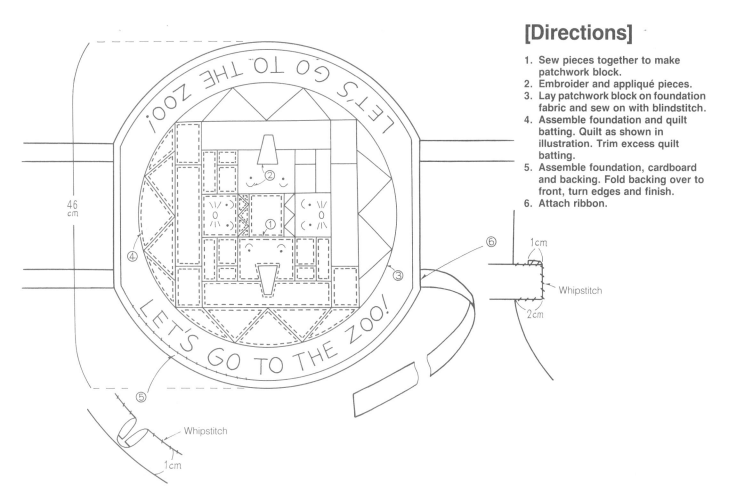

[Directions]

1. Sew pieces together to make patchwork block.
2. Embroider and appliqué pieces.
3. Lay patchwork block on foundation fabric and sew on with blindstitch.
4. Assemble foundation and quilt batting. Quilt as shown in illustration. Trim excess quilt batting.
5. Assemble foundation, cardboard and backing. Fold backing over to front, turn edges and finish.
6. Attach ribbon.

[Piecing]   Add 0.7cm seam allowance and cut pieces.

[Piecing Diagram]

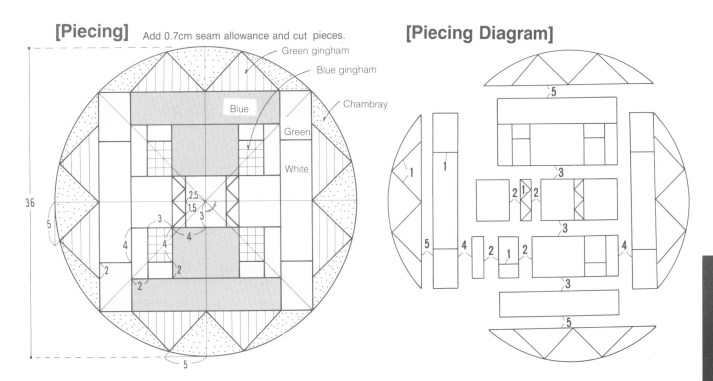

ANIMAL PATCHWORK
CAT

Cat Apron

Instructions on page 65.

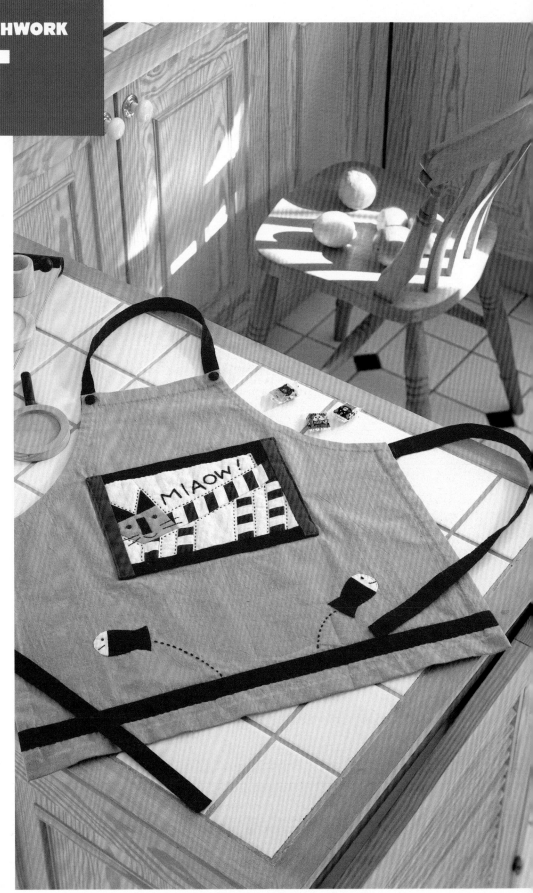

P. 64 Cat Apron

[Materials]

Mustard color cotton fabric—65cm × 55cm
Red cotton fabric—55cm × 40cm
White cotton fabric—30cm × 20cm
Red & White striped cotton fabric—15cm square
Dark brown cotton fabric—10cm × 20cm
Lightweight quilt batting—25cm × 20cm
Red and White quilting thread
#25 Red, White, Dark brown embroidery floss
2 Red buttons (1.3cm in diameter)
1 pair large snaps

[Drafting and Cutting]

Add seam allowance indicated in parenthesis and cut pieces.
Cut 1 quilt batting 23cm × 17cm.

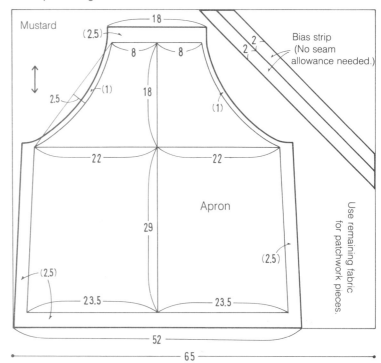

Border (Add 1cm seam allowance.)

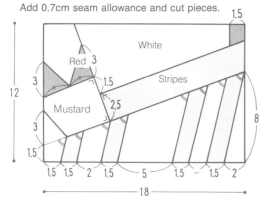

[Piecing]

Add 0.7cm seam allowance and cut pieces.

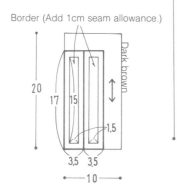

[Piecing Diagram]

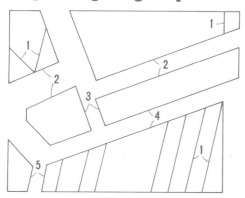

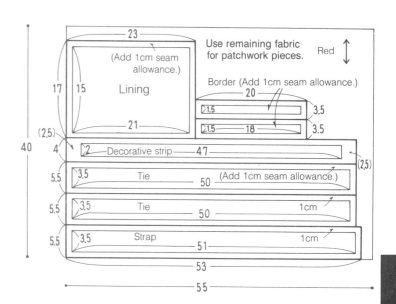

[Directions]

1. Sew pieces together to make patchwork block. (Iron seams towards motif so that design will show up.)
2. Sew on borders.
3. Embroider and appliqué pieces.
4. With right sides together, place patchwork block on lining and lay on batting. Sew around block and turn inside out. Whipstitch opening.
5. Quilt using 3 strands of red embroidery floss.
6. Sew pocket onto apron using red quilting thread and sew with half backstitch.
7. Whipstitch decorative strip and stay stitch using a running stitch.
8. Finish edge of apron bib with bias strip.
9. Sew ties.
10. Turn edges, insert ties and finish edges.
11. Sew on buttons.
12. Sew on snaps.

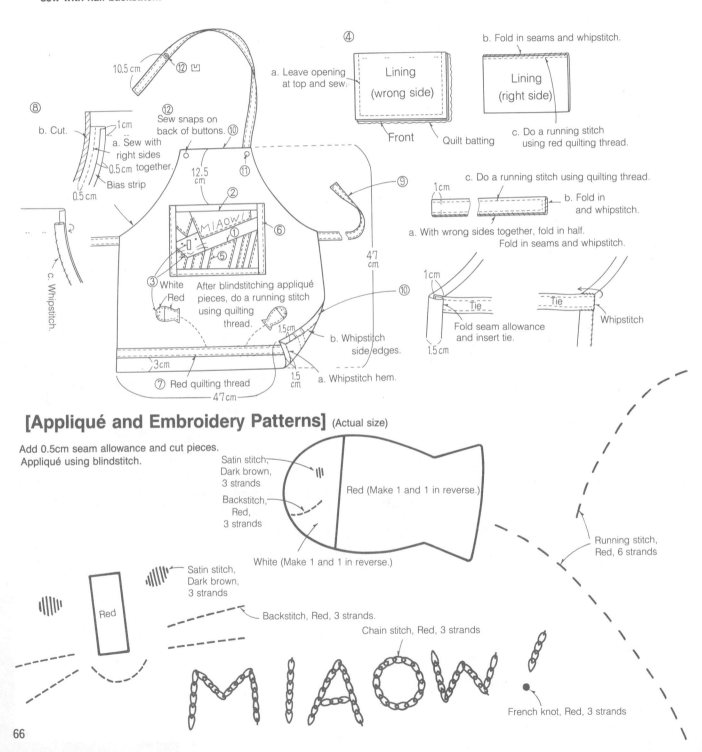

10.5 cm ⑫

⑧
b. Cut.
1cm
a. Sew with right sides together.
0.5cm
Bias strip
0.5cm
c. Whipstitch.

Sew snaps on back of buttons. ⑩
⑫
⑪
12.5 cm

④
a. Leave opening at top and sew.
Lining (wrong side)
Front   Quilt batting

b. Fold in seams and whipstitch.
Lining (right side)
c. Do a running stitch using red quilting thread.

②
①
③ White
Red
⑥
⑤
MIAOW!
After blindstitching appliqué pieces, do a running stitch using quilting thread.

⑨
47 cm
⑩
1.5cm
b. Whipstitch side edges.
3cm
⑦ Red quilting thread
47cm
1.5 cm
a. Whipstitch hem.

1cm
c. Do a running stitch using quilting thread.
b. Fold in and whipstitch.
a. With wrong sides together, fold in half.
Fold in seams and whipstitch.

1cm
Tie
Fold seam allowance and insert tie.
1.5 cm

Tie
Whipstitch

[Appliqué and Embroidery Patterns] (Actual size)

Add 0.5cm seam allowance and cut pieces.
Appliqué using blindstitch.

Satin stitch, Dark brown, 3 strands
Backstitch, Red, 3 strands
Red (Make 1 and 1 in reverse.)
White (Make 1 and 1 in reverse.)

Running stitch, Red, 6 strands

Satin stitch, Dark brown, 3 strands
Red
Backstitch, Red, 3 strands.
Chain stitch, Red, 3 strands
MIAOW!
French knot, Red, 3 strands

Continued from P. 7

[Eagle]   ⑤ Quilting pattern

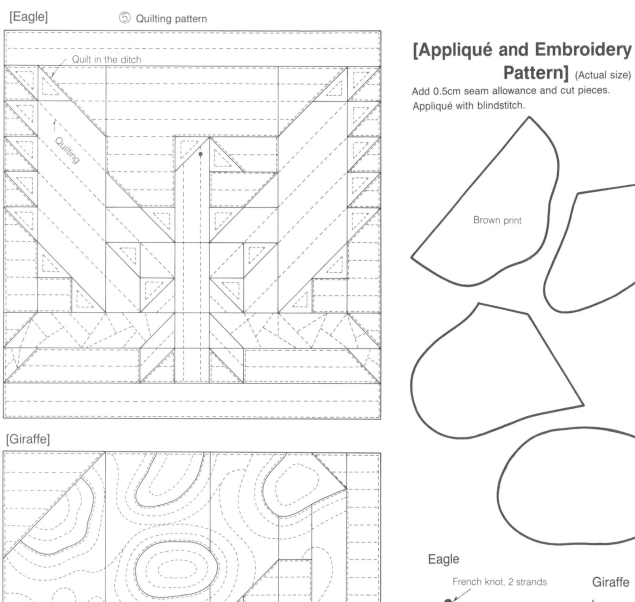

Quilt in the ditch

Quilting

[Giraffe]

Quilting

Quilt in the ditch

[Appliqué and Embroidery Pattern] (Actual size)

Add 0.5cm seam allowance and cut pieces.
Appliqué with blindstitch.

Brown print

Eagle

French knot, 2 strands

Giraffe

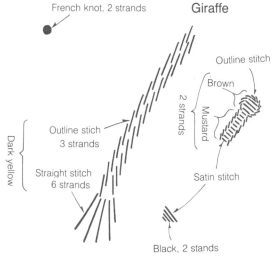

Outline stitch

Brown

2 strands

Mustard

Dark yellow

Outline stich
3 strands

Straight stitch
6 strands

Satin stitch

Black, 2 stands

P. 12 Whale Drawstring Bags

[Materials]
[Large]

Heart print on off-white cotton fabric—60cm × 40cm
Dark brown flower print cotton fabric—20cm square
Cotton backing fabric—55cm × 30cm
Quilt batting—55cm × 30cm
25 Black embroidery floss
2 Off-white cords (chemically treated) (0.3cm in diameter,
60cm long)

[Small]

Heart print on off-white cotton fabric—30cm square
Red flower print cotton fabric—20cm square
Cotton backing fabric—35cm × 20cm
Quilt batting—35cm × 20cm
25 Black embroidery floss
2 Off-white cords (chemically treated) (0.3cm in diameter,
50cm long)

[Directions]
[Large]

1. Sew pieces together to make patchwork block.
2. With right sides together, sew border A.
3. With right sides together, sew border B.
4. Assemble patchwork block and quilt batting. Quilt in
   the ditch.
5. Quilt 2.2cm wide lines all over patchwork block as
   shown in illustration.
6. Embroider.
7. Trace whale shape on back fabric. Assemble back
   fabric and quilt batting. Quilt using the same off-white
   quilting thread used for quilting in the ditch on the front.
8. Quilt as in (5).
9. Assemble backing, front and back as shown in illustration
   and sew. Turn inside out.
10. Sew top strips A and then B.
11. With right sides together, sew bag and top strips.
12. Fold top strip at fold line. Whipstitch edge so that
    stitches will not show on the front.
13. Machine stitch.
14. Insert 2 cords and tie ends.

[Small]

Make small bag following instructions for large bag but omit the border strips.

[Drafting and Cutting]

Add 1cm seam allowance and cut pieces.

Cut 2 each of quilt batting and backing
[Large] in the following measurements: 27cm square.

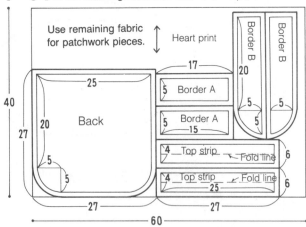

[Small] Cut 2 each of quilt batting and backing
in the following measurements
17cm square.

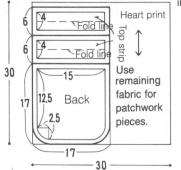

[Piecing] Add 0.7cm seam allowance and cut pieces.

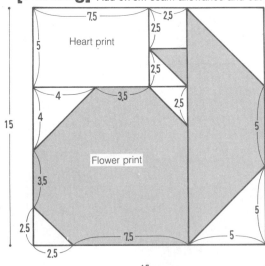

[Piecing Diagram]

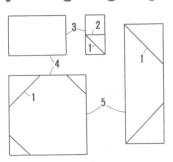

68

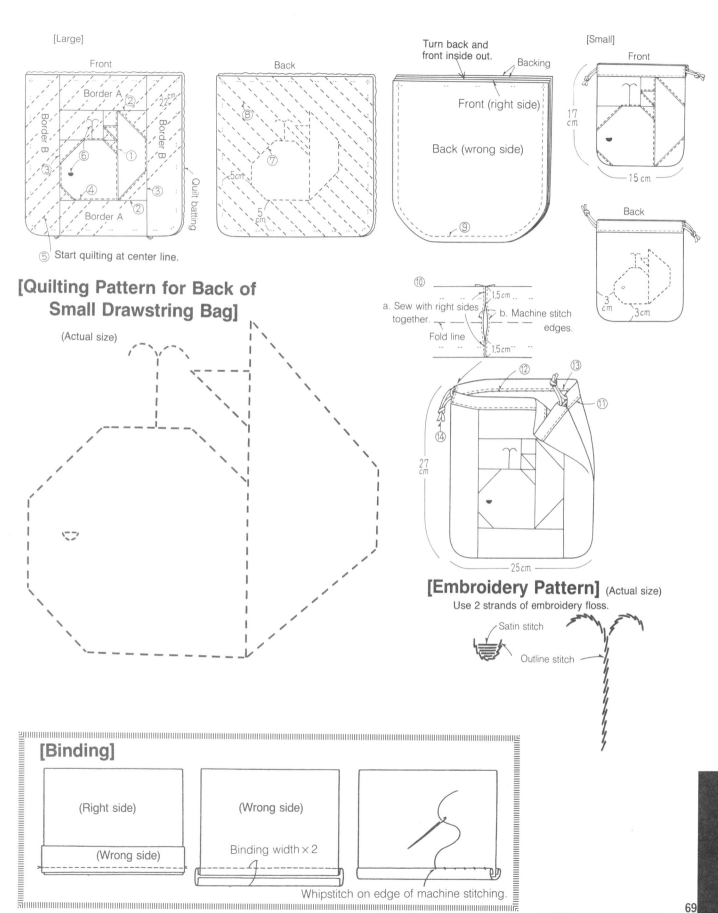

[Large]

Front

Border A
②
2 cm
22 cm

Border B

Border B

⑥
①

③
④

③

②

Border A

⑤ Start quilting at center line.

Quilt batting

Back

⑧

⑦

5 cm

5 cm

Turn back and
front inside out.

Backing

Front (right side)

Back (wrong side)

⑨

[Small]

Front

17 cm

15 cm

Back

3 cm

3 cm

[Quilting Pattern for Back of Small Drawstring Bag]

(Actual size)

⑩
1.5 cm
a. Sew with right sides
together.
b. Machine stitch
edges.
Fold line
1.5 cm

⑫ ⑬

⑪

⑭

27 cm

25 cm

[Embroidery Pattern] (Actual size)
Use 2 strands of embroidery floss.

Satin stitch

Outline stitch

[Binding]

(Right side)

(Wrong side)

(Wrong side)

Binding width × 2

Whipstitch on edge of machine stitching.

69

Continued from P. 11

[Lunch Bag]

1. Sew pieces together to make patchwork block.
2. Sew patchwork block and A.
3. Sew (2) and B.
4. Assemble (2) and quilt batting. Quilt as shown in illustration.
5. Embroider and appliqué pieces.
6. Sew A and B for back.
7. Assemble A and quilt batting. Quilt as shown in illustration.
8. Machine stitch 0.2cm on outer edge of finished line of A.
9. Assemble outer sole, quilt batting and inner sole. Machine stitch 0.2cm on outer edge of finished line.
10. With right sides together, sew side seams of front and back, leaving seams of cord casement unsewn.
11. With right sides together, sew (9) and (10).
12. With right sides together, sew side seams of backing.
13. With right sides together, sew opening and turn inside out.
14. Whipstitch lining to sole.
15. Sew cord casement and insert cotton cords.

[Shoe Bag]

1. Sew pieces together to make patchwork block.
2. Sew patchwork block and border A.
3. Sew (2) and border B.
4. Sew (3) and top and bottom strips.
5. Assemble patchwork block and quilt batting. Quilt as shown in illustration.
6. Embroider and appliqué pieces.
7. Sew back and top and bottom strips.
8. Assemble (7) and quilt batting. Quilt as shown in illustration.
9. Machine stitch 0.2cm on outer edge of finished line.
10. With right sides together, sew front and back.
11. Make gusset.
12. With right sides together, fold backing and sew side seams. Refer to (11) and make gusset. Turn inside out.
13. Refer to bag and make handle.
14. Make loop.
15. With wrong sides together, sew (10) and (12) at top edge, inserting handle and loop.

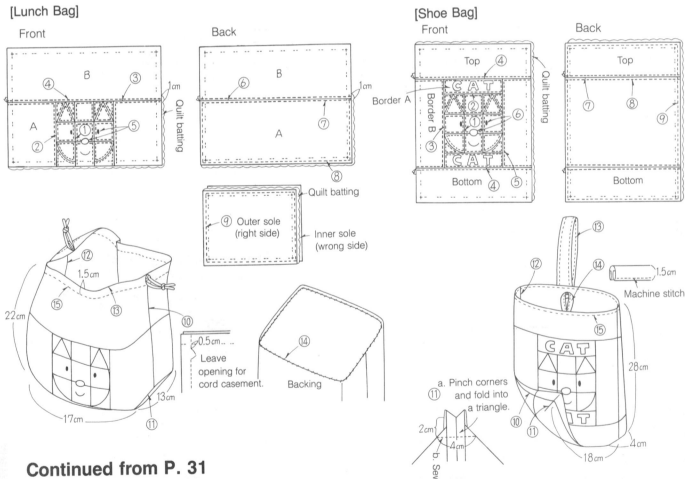

Continued from P. 31

7. With right sides together, sew front and back at side seams and bottom seams. Finish seam edges.
8. Make gusset and sew on tape.
9. Turn bag inside out. Sew bias strip at top edge. (Refer to P. 69.)
10. Whipstitch off-white lace on edge of binding.
11. Make handles and attach.
12. Make embellishment and attach.
13. Attach magnet snaps.

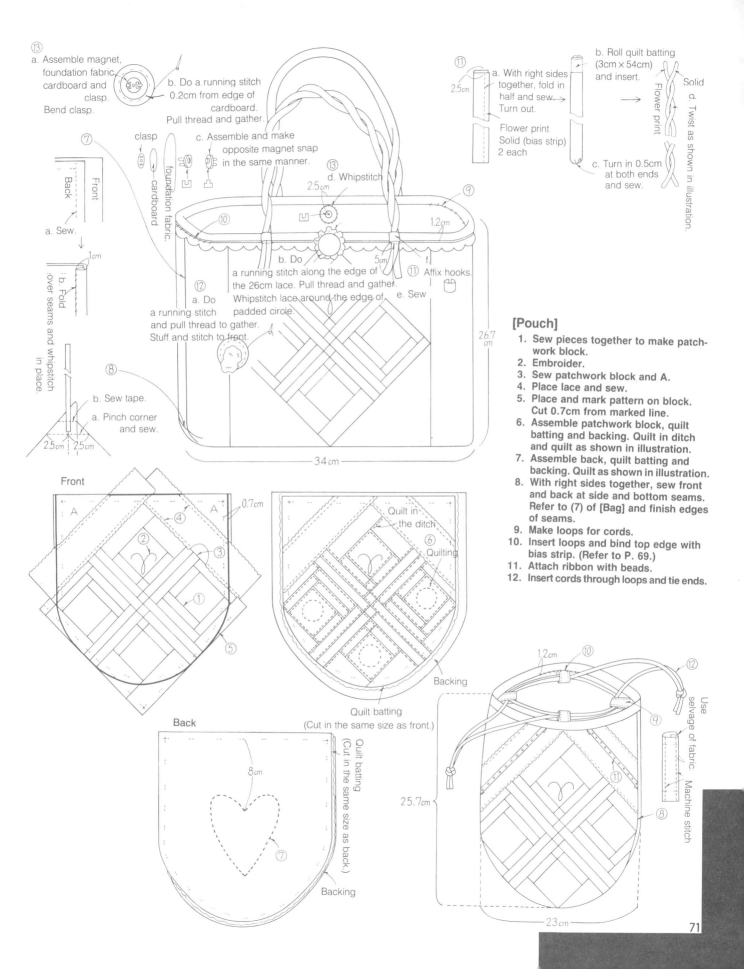

⑬
a. Assemble magnet, foundation fabric, cardboard and clasp. Bend clasp.

b. Do a running stitch 0.2cm from edge of cardboard. Pull thread and gather.

c. Assemble and make opposite magnet snap in the same manner.

⑦
Back Front
a. Sew.

1cm
b. Fold over seams and whipstitch in place.

clasp
foundation fabric. cardboard

⑬ Whipstitch
2.5cm
d. Whipstitch

⑩

b. Do a running stitch along the edge of the 26cm lace. Pull thread and gather. Whipstitch lace around the edge of padded circle.

⑫
a. Do a running stitch and pull thread to gather. Stuff and stitch to front.

e. Sew
5cm
⑪
f. Affix hooks.

⑨
1.2cm

26.7cm

⑧
b. Sew tape.
a. Pinch corner and sew.
2.5cm 2.5cm

34cm

⑪
2.5cm
a. With right sides together, fold in half and sew. Turn out.

Flower print Solid (bias strip) 2 each

b. Roll quilt batting (3cm × 54cm) and insert.

c. Turn in 0.5cm at both ends and sew.

Solid
Flower print
d. Twist as shown in illustration.

Front
A   A
0.7cm
④
②
③
①
⑤

Quilt in the ditch
⑥ Quilting

Backing
Quilt batting (Cut in the same size as front.)

Back
8cm
⑦
Quilt batting (Cut in the same size as back.)
Backing

[Pouch]
1. Sew pieces together to make patch-work block.
2. Embroider.
3. Sew patchwork block and A.
4. Place lace and sew.
5. Place and mark pattern on block. Cut 0.7cm from marked line.
6. Assemble patchwork block, quilt batting and backing. Quilt in ditch and quilt as shown in illustration.
7. Assemble back, quilt batting and backing. Quilt as shown in illustration.
8. With right sides together, sew front and back at side and bottom seams. Refer to (7) of [Bag] and finish edges of seams.
9. Make loops for cords.
10. Insert loops and bind top edge with bias strip. (Refer to P. 69.)
11. Attach ribbon with beads.
12. Insert cords through loops and tie ends.

1.2cm
⑩
⑫
Use selvage of fabric. Machine stitch
⑨
⑪
25.7cm
⑧
23cm

71

P. 25 Monster Bag with Pencil Case

[Materials]

Black cotton fabric—60cm square
Red gingham fabric—90cm × 30cm
Red cotton fabric—40cm × 35cm
Mustard cotton fabric—40cm × 30cm
Blue flower print fabric—30cm × 25cm

Green cotton fabric—30cm × 20cm
Cotton fabric scraps in Blue, Charcoal gray, Pink, Light blue, etc.
Black felt scraps
Quilt batting—80cm × 40cm
1 Black zipper (10cm long)

[Drafting and Cutting]

Add seam allowance indicated in parenthesis and cut pieces.

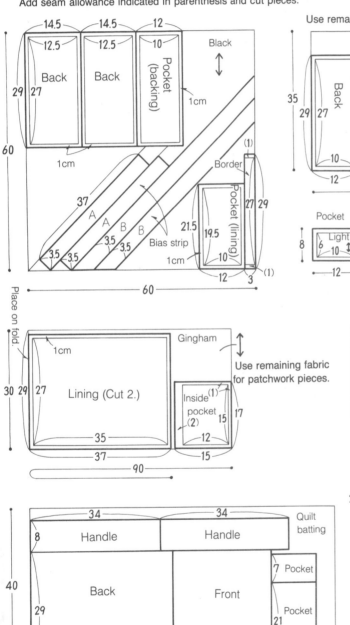

Use remaining fabric for patchwork pieces.

[Piecing Diagram]

[Piecing]

Add 0.7cm seam allowance and cut pieces.

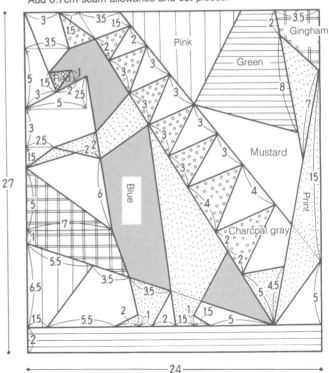

[Directions]

1. Sew pieces together to make patchwork block. Assemble block and quilt batting. Quilt in the ditch as shown in illustration. Appliqué the piece for "eye."
2. Assemble pocket and quilt batting and quilt. Attach zipper to lower half and sew on backing. Lay pocket on pocket lining and attach upper half of zipper. Baste around pocket.
3. Join (1) and (2) to border strip.
4. Quilt along side border with black thread.
5. Assemble front and lining with wrong sides together. Bind top edge with bias strip A. (Refer to P. 69.)
6. Sew inside pocket to remaining lining piece.
7. Piece back.
8. Assemble back and quilt batting. Quilt as shown in illustration using specified thread.
9. Assemble back and (6) with wrong sides together. Bind top edge with bias strip A.
10. Assemble front and back with wrong sides together. Bind around edge with bias B.
11. Make handles and attach to bag.

[Pattern]
(Actual size)

No seam allowance needed.
Sew on appliqué piece with blindstitch.

Felt

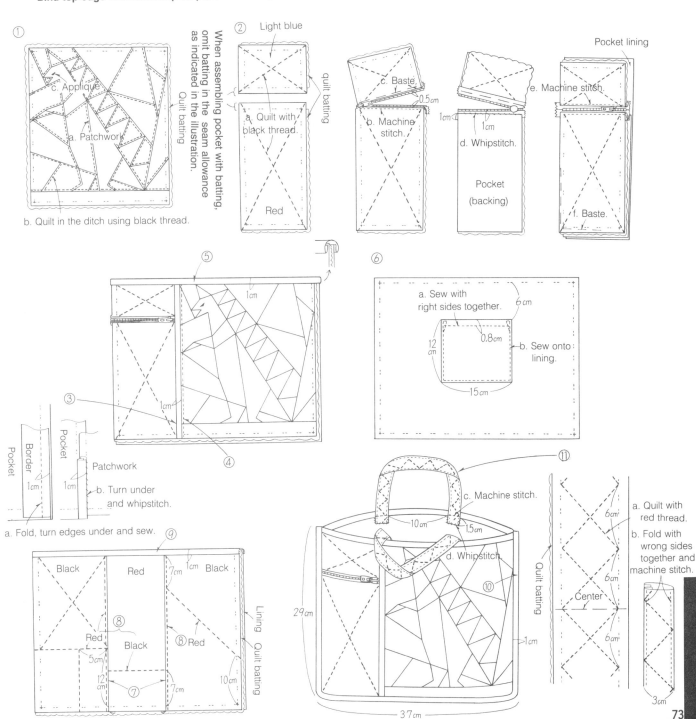

73

P. 44 Cat Cushions

[Materials]
[Materials needed for both cushions]

(Yardage for 1 cushion)

Cotton fabric for back—
50cm × 40cm
Cotton backing fabric—
50cm × 35cm
Quilt batting—50cm square
Zipper (38cm long)
Uncovered cushion—
46cm × 32cm

[Cat on left]

Beige print fabric—45cm × 40cm
Gray print fabric—30cm × 25cm
Dark beige print fabric—
25cm × 15cm
Black print fabric—15cm square
Gray-brown and white plaid
scraps
Print scraps for patchwork block:
Brown, Red, Brown & Dark
yellow, Dark yellow, White,
reddish-brown, green
#25 Embroidery floss in the
following colors: Black, Gray,
Charcoal gray, Red.

[Cat on right]

Light blue print fabric—40cm square
White print fabric—25cm × 30cm
Brown print fabric—20cm square
Brown & black print fabric—15cm × 20cm
Dark yellow print fabric—15cm square
Gray-brown print fabric—15cm square
Brown check fabric—10cm square
Gray print fabric scraps
Charcoal gray print fabric scraps
#25 Gray-brown, Black, Charcoal Gray
embroidery floss

[Directions]

1. Make tail and ears of mouse. Appliqué fish fins.
2. Sew pieces together to make patchwork block.
3. Embroider.
4. Assemble patchwork block, quilt batting and backing. Quilt in the ditch and quilt as shown in illustration.
5. Stitch the ends of cat's tail and both ends of mouse's tail to patchwork block.
6. Refer to [Elephant] and [Rabbit] (P. 46) for instructions on finishing cushion.

[Finished size]

44cm × 33cm

Left [Piecing]
Add 0.7cm seam allowance and cut pieces.
Cut 1 each of quilt batting and backing in the following measurements: 46cm × 32cm.

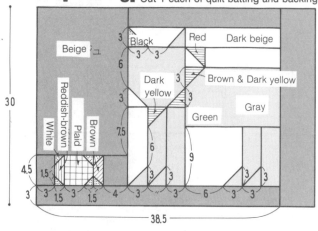

[Piecing Diagram]

Left

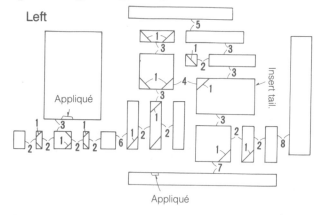

Right

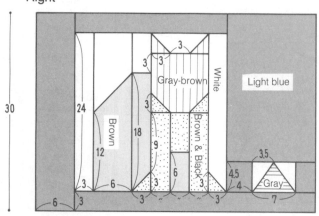

Right

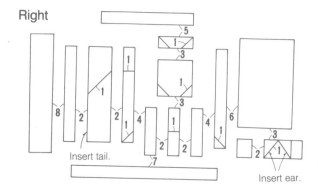

[Drafting and Cutting]

Add seam allowance indicated in parenthesis and cut pieces.

Cotton fabric for back

(1) (1)
Back
Zipper placement
13.5
10
3 3 3

40 (2.5)

Zipper placement
3 3
23.5
20
Back

(1)
(1)
44
46
50

Left Black print fabric
Right Dark yellow print fabric
Use remaining black fabric
for patchwork pieces.

Brown check
10
3
7.5
Mouse's tail
(No seam allowance needed.)
10

15
6
Tail
(No seam allowance needed.)
15

[Patterns, Appliqué and Embroidery Patterns] (Actual size)

Add 0.5cm seam allowance to patterns and cut pieces.
Add 0.5cm seam allowance to appliqué pieces.
Sew on using blindstitch.

[Left]

[Right] Stitch on to block. ⑤

2.5cm
3cm
④ Quilt
④
Quilt in the ditch
indicated in bold lines.
③
③
①
③ Quilt print pattern
of gray fabric.
④
1.5 cm
⑥
② Insert tail and piece patchwork block.

Cat's tail on
left is 15cm;
right is 13cm.

0.5cm
2cm
b. Cut.

a. Fold in half with
right sides together
and sew.

c. Insert batting
in the following
measurements.
Width: 17cm
Length: (left) 14cm
(right) 12cm

[Right]
Quilt
1cm
2 2 2
2
0.5
④ Quilt print pattern in brown fabric.
⑥
③
④ Quilt in the ditch indicated in bold lines.
②
⑤ Stitch onto block.

① For cat's tail, refer
to above illustration.
Mouse's tail
0.5 cm
a. Fold in half with
right sides together
and sew.
b. Turn inside out.
Insert quilt batting cut
to 1.5cm × 6.5cm
and rolled.
c. Turn in 0.5cm
at both ends and stitch.
With right sides together,
sew 2 and turn inside out.

② Insert "tail" and mouse's "ear" and
piece patchwork block.

Outline stitch
Gray-brown, 1 strand

[Left]
Fish
Fin
Brown
Do not stitch here.
Brown
Outline stitch, 3 strands
Gray Black

Eye
Bullion knot
Use 2 strands of black floss.
Mouth
Outline stitch
Use 2 strands of red floss.

[Right]
Outline stitch
Black, 3 strands
Black
French knot
1 strand
Outline stitch
2 strands

Satin stitch Outline stitch
Charcoal gray, 3 strands

[Mouse]
Eye
Bullion knot
Use 2 strands of black floss.

Ear
Make 4.
Charcoal gray
Opening

Satin stitch Outline stitch
Charcoal gray, 3 strands

75

P. 44 Dog Mini-cushion

[Materials]

Black and Dark brown plaid fabric—35cm × 20cm
Brown print fabric—30cm × 15cm
White print fabric—25cm square
Print fabric scraps for patchwork (Refer to photo.)
Cotton fabric for back—40cm × 35cm
Cotton backing fabric—35cm square
Quilt batting—35cm square
1 Zipper (27cm long)
1 Black button (1cm in diameter)
Uncovered cushion—33cm square

[Directions]

1. Make "ear." Appliqué "nose."
2. Sew pieces together to make patchwork block.
3. Assemble patchwork block, quilt batting and backing. Quilt in the ditch and quilt as shown in illustration.
4. Attach button.
5. Finish cushion referring to the directions given for [Elephant] and [Rabbit] cushions. (P. 46)

[Finished size]

31cm square

[Piecing]

Add 0.7cm seam allowance and cut pieces.
Cut 1 each of quilt batting and backing
in the following measurement: 33cm square.

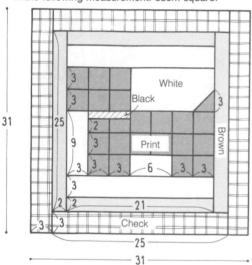

[Drafting and Cutting]

Add seam allowance indicated in parenthesis and cut pieces.

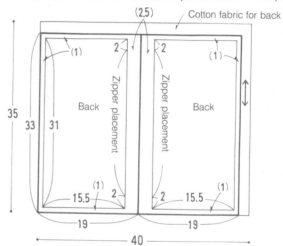

[Piecing Diagram]

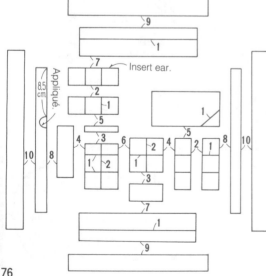

Insert ear.

[Pattern and Appliqué Pattern]

(Actual size)
Add 0.5cm seam allowance
and cut pieces.

Opening
Ear
Cut 2.
Check

Nose
Black
Do not stitch.
Blindstitch

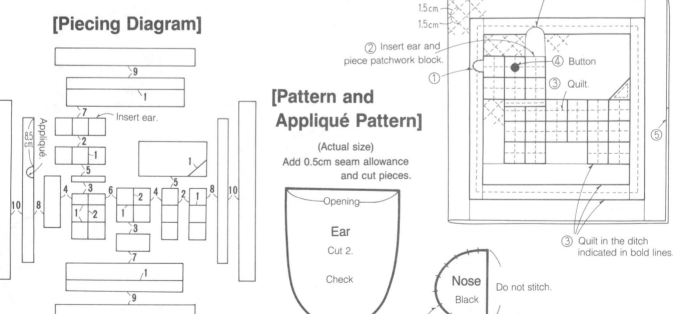

① Sew with right sides together and turn inside out.
② Insert ear and piece patchwork block.
③ Quilt.
④ Button
⑤
③ Quilt in the ditch indicated in bold lines.

Continued from P. 39

[Mat]

1. Sew pieces together to make patchwork block.
2. Sew "sheep" block and border A, B, C following instructions given from (a) through (c).
3. Embroider and appliqué pieces.
4. Sew on pieced border.
5. Sew (4) and border D, E following instructions given in (a) and (b).
6. Appliqué "flag" and "pole" pieces.

7. With right sides together, sew center seam of backing.
8. Assemble top, quilt batting and backing. Quilt as shown in illustration.
9. Refer to (11) of [Bed Quilt] and finish seam edges.
10. Make wheels and attach.
11. Attach ribbon.

[Mat]

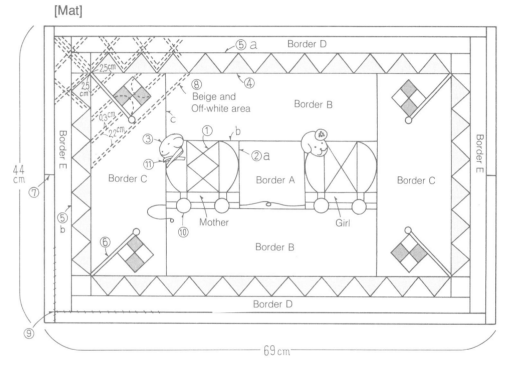

Flag pole

[Appliqué and Embroidery Patterns] (Actual size)

Add 0.5cm seam allowance and cut pieces. Sew on appliqué pieces with blindstitch.
Use 3 strands for embroidery.

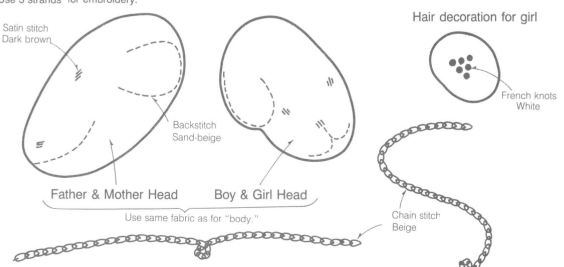

Satin stitch
Dark brown

Backstitch
Sand-beige

Hair decoration for girl

French knots
White

Father & Mother Head

Boy & Girl Head

Use same fabric as for "body."

Chain stitch
Beige

Check

Make 4 each.

P. 49 Rabbit, Cat, Monkey and Elephant Wall Pocket

[Materials]

Off-white pre-quilted fabric—85cm × 25cm
Off-white cotton fabric—85cm × 10cm
Cotton fabric scraps for patchwork in Pinks, Greens, Browns and Blues (Refer to photo.)
Cotton backing fabric—90cm × 20cm
Quilt battig—90cm × 20cm
#25 embroidery floss in Yellow-green, Brick-red, Bright pink, Moss green, Green, Dark brown, Brown, Blue
White quilting thread
Pink satin ribbon (0.6cm wide, 55cm long)
Polyester stuffing
2 Wooden hangers

[Directions]

1. Appliqué.
2. Make elephant's nose.
3. Sew pieces together to make patchwork block.
4. Assemble (3) and quilt batting. With right sides together, lay backing on (3). Sew top and bottom edges. Turn inside out.
5. Embroider and attach "nose."
6. Quilt as shown in illustration.
7. Sew bottom edge of pocket to foundation. Baste sides to foundation.
8. Bind both sides. (Refer to P. 69.) Embroider.
9. Embroider foundation.
10. Fold at fold line. Turn under edges and stitch as shown in illustration. Insert hangers.
11. Tie ribbon to hanger.

[Drafting and Cutting]
Add seam allowance indicated in parenthesis and cut pieces.

Cut 4 each of quilt batting and backing in the following measurement: 20cm × 17cm.

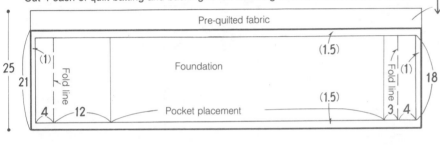

[Piecing Diagram]

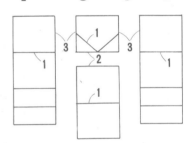

[Piecing]

Add 1cm seam allowance and cut pieces.

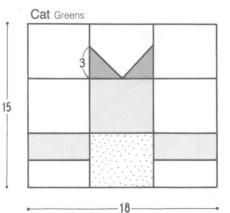

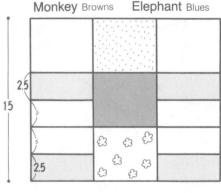

[Appliqué and Embroidery Patterns] (Actual size)

Add 1cm seam allowance and cut pieces. Sew on using blindstitch.
Use 3 strands of embroidery floss.

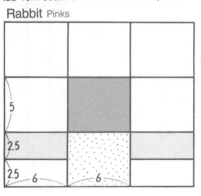

Yellow-green   Brick-red
Chain stitch

ToTEMPOLE

Monkey's ear and face
Make elephant's ear in the same way.
a. Blindstitch appliqué piece.

b. Leave 0.3cm seam allowance
and trim away excess
foundation fabric.

⑤ Nose
Stuffing
For "rabbit" and "cat", use
4cm (in diameter) circle.
For "monkey", use
3cm (in diameter) circle.
Do a running stitch 0.5cm from edge.
Place stuffing and gather.

Elephant

Ear (Cut 2.)

Nose

(Cut 1 and
1 in reverse.)

|||

Monkey

Ear
(Cut 2.)

Satin stitch
Backstitch
} Dark
brown

Running stitch
dark brown.

Rabbit

Ear (Cut 2.)

Bright pink
Backstitch   Satin stitch

||| |||

① ④
0.5cm
0.5cm
Quilting
thread
⑥
⑤
Bright pink
3 strands
③

Quilting
thread
Green
3 strands

Quilting
thread
Brown
3 strands

Quilting thread
Blue
3 strands
Insert when piecing
patchwork block.

②

a. Sew with
right sides
together.

Quilt batting

b. Trim seam
allowance to 0.3cm.
Turn inside out.

Cat
Moss green
{ Backstitch
Satin stitch

Patchwork block
(right side)
Quilt batting
Backing (wrong side)

4cm
⑩ ⑪

3cm
⑨
TOTEMPOLE
3cm
⑧
1.5cm

⑦

75cm

Use 3 strans of yellow-green embroidery floss
and do a running stitch

21cm

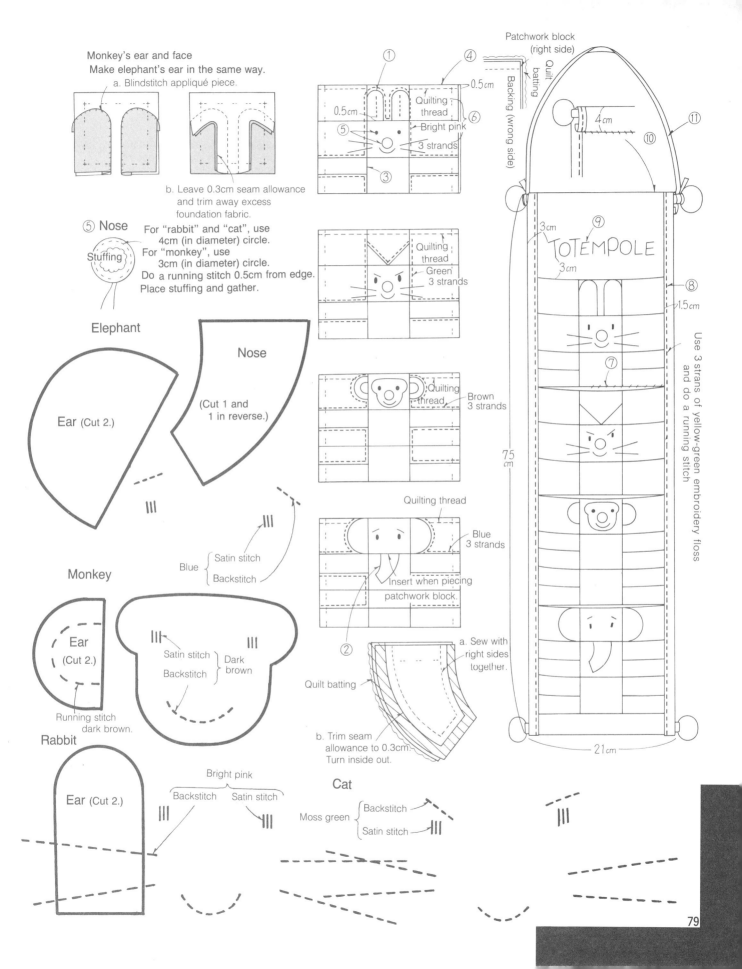

Continued from P. 43

[Directions]
[Bed Quilt]

1. Sew pieces together to make patchwork blocks.
2. Lay border A on quilt batting. With right sides together, place patchwork block A on border A and sew. Open block A.
3. Sew border B, block B, border C ...... in the same way as in (2).
4. Quilt as shown in illustration.
5. Sew on patchwork border. Quilt as shown in illustration.
6. With right sides together, sew center seam of backing.

7. With right sides together, sew top and backing leaving an opening. Turn inside out and sew opening.
8. Tie at the 13 marks to hold quilt in place.
9. Sew around edges of backing so that stitches will not show on front. (Refer to P. 27.)

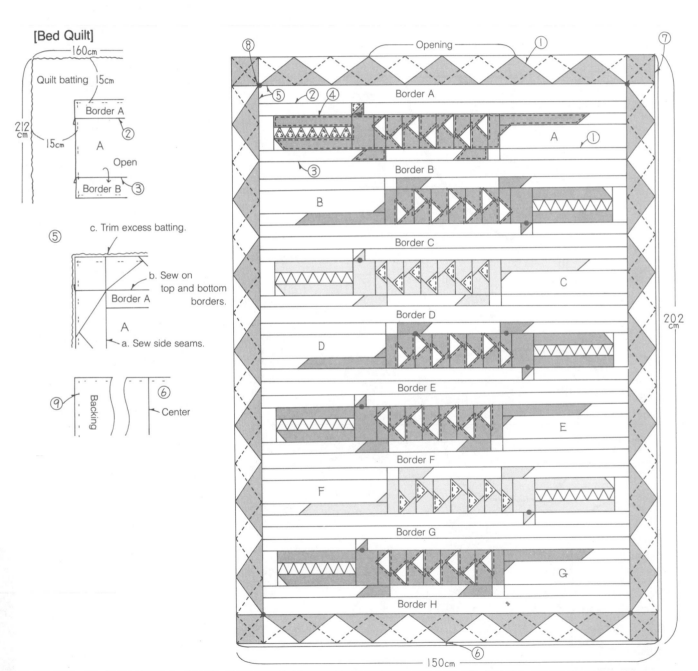

[Pajama Bag]

1. Sew pieces together to make patchwork block.
2. Sew patchwork block and border A, B.
3. Assemble patchwork block and quilt batting. Quilt as shown in illustration.
4. Assemble outer sole and quilt batting. Quilt as shown in illustration.
5. With right sides together, sew side seams of side panel and of backing to make a tube.
6. Sew side panel to outer sole; lining to inner sole.
7. Sew opening strip.
8. Sew side panel, lining and opening strip together.
9. Insert cotton cords and tie ends.

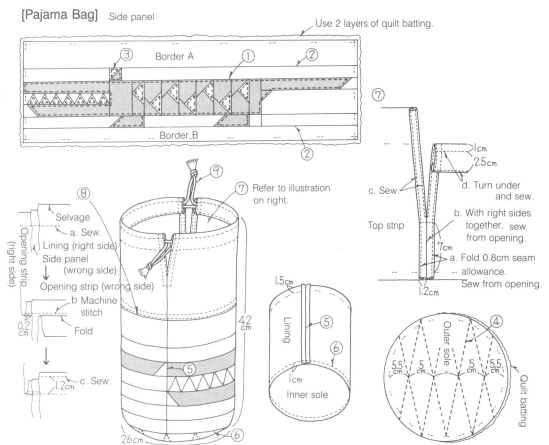

[Pajama Bag] Side panel

Use 2 layers of quilt batting.

Border A ① ②

③

⑦

Border B ②

⑨

⑧

⑦ Refer to illustration on right.

Selvage
a. Sew.
Lining (right side)
Side panel (wrong side)
Opening strip (wrong side)
b Machine stitch
Fold
0.2 cm
c. Sew.
1.2 cm
Opening strip (right side)

1 cm
2.5 cm
c. Sew.
d. Turn under and sew.
Top strip
b. With right sides together, sew from opening.
7cm
a. Fold 0.8cm seam allowance. Sew from opening.
1.2cm

42 cm
⑤
26cm
⑥

1.5cm
Lining
⑤
⑥
1cm
Inner sole

④
Outer sole
5.5 cm 5 cm 5 cm 5.5 cm
Quilt batting

P. 53 Stuffed Terrier Toys

[Materials]
[Large]

Cotton scraps in navy blues for patchwork blocks—You will need 84 squares that are 4.4cm square.
2 Black buttons (0.7cm in diameter)
Satin ribbon (0.9cm wide, 50cm long)
Polyester stuffing

[Small]

Cotton scraps in navy blues and reds for patchwork blocks—You will need 84 squares that are 3.4cm square.
2 Black buttons (0.7cm in diameter)
Satin ribbon (0.5cm wide, 35cm long)
Polyester stuffing

[Directions]

1. Piece side panel as shown in illustration.
2. For gusset, piece 30 blocks in one row.
3. Sew side panel and gusset together. Leave opening.
4. Stuff with polyester stuffing and stitch opening.
5. Attach eyes.
6. Tie ribbon.

[Pattern] (Actual size)

Add 0.7cm seam allowance and cut 84 squares.

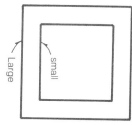

Large

small

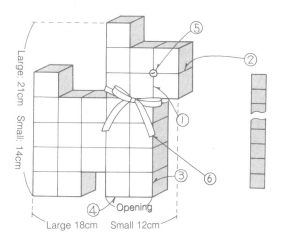

⑤
②
①
③
⑥
④ Opening
Large: 21cm Small: 14cm
Large 18cm Small 12cm

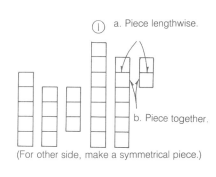

① a. Piece lengthwise.

b. Piece together.

(For other side, make a symmetrical piece.)

P. 61 Terrier and Cat Mini-buckets

[Materials]
[Terrier]

Black broadcloth—70cm × 35cm
Crimson print fabric—30cm square
Cotton backing fabric—50cm × 30cm
Quilt batting—70cm × 30cm
1 Cardboard (11cm in diameter)
2 Crimson satin ribbon (0.4cm wide, 23cm long)
2 Blue beads (0.3cm in diameter)
4 Black beads (0.3cm in diameter)

[Cat]

Beige paisley print fabric—70cm × 35cm
Off-white broadcloth—30cm square
Printed fabric scraps: Brown, Light brown, Browns, Beige, Off-white and
Crimson, Mustard, Red, Green, Brown & Off-white stripes
Cotton backing fabric—50cm × 30cm
Quilt batting—70cm × 30cm
1 Cardboard (11cm in diameter)
Off-white cluny lace (2cm wide, 42cm long)
2 Off-white satin ribbon (0.3cm wide, 16cm long)
2 Pearl beads (0.3cm in diameter)
2 Bells (1cm in diameter)

[Directions]

1. Sew pieces to make patchwork block.
2. With right sides together, sew patchwork motif and gusset.
3. Assemble outer panel, quilt batting (50cm × 30cm) and backing. Baste the 3 layers. Leave 5cm around the edge and trim excess fabric and batting. Quilt as shown in illustration.
4. Leave 2cm seam allowance on backing side seams of gusset. Trim quilt batting and backing seam allowance to the size of the outer panel.
5. Sew side seams and finish edges.
6. Bind top and bottom edges with bias strips. (Refer to P. 69.)
7. Sew sole.
8. Make handles and attach to bag.

[Drafting and Cutting]

Add seam allowance indicated in parenthesis and cut pieces.

Cut 1 backing: 50cm × 30cm
Cutting 1 quilt batting each in the following sizes: 50cm × 30cm, 7cm × 30cm, 11cm in diameter.

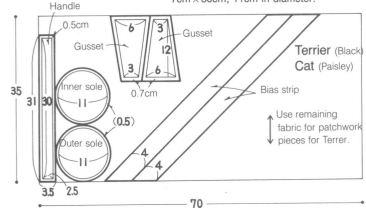

[Piecing]

Add 0.7cm seam allowance and cut pieces.

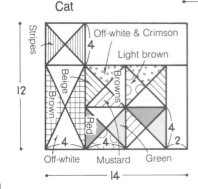

[Piecing Diagram]

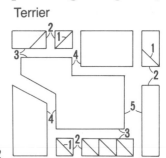

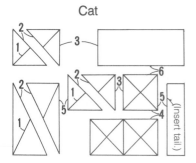

[Appliqué Pattern] (Actual size)
Add 0.5cm seam allowance and cut piece.
Sew on appliqué piece using blindstitch.

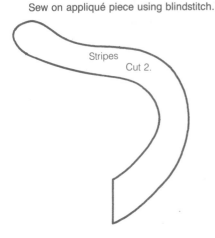

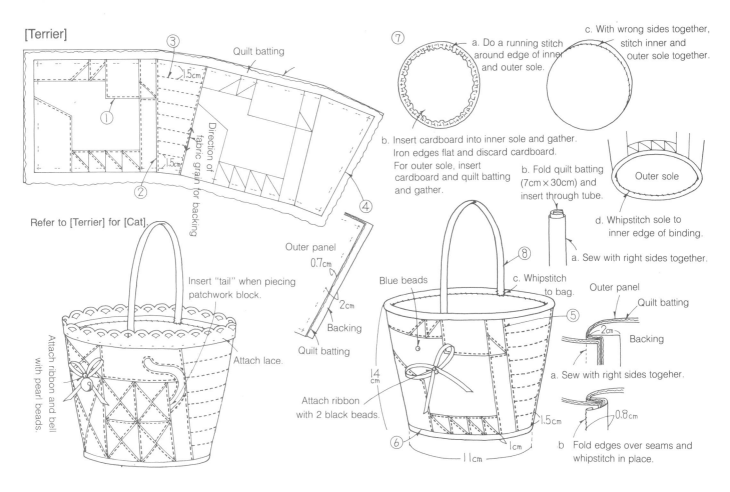

[Terrier]

Quilt batting

③

1.5cm

1.5cm

①

②

Direction of fabric grain for backing

⑦ a. Do a running stitch around edge of inner and outer sole.

c. With wrong sides together, stitch inner and outer sole together.

b. Insert cardboard into inner sole and gather. Iron edges flat and discard cardboard. For outer sole, insert cardboard and quilt batting and gather.

b. Fold quilt batting (7cm × 30cm) and insert through tube.

Outer sole

d. Whipstitch sole to inner edge of binding.

a. Sew with right sides together.

Refer to [Terrier] for [Cat].

Insert "tail" when piecing patchwork block.

Attach lace.

Attach ribbon and bell with pearl beads.

④

Outer panel
0.7cm

2cm

Backing

Quilt batting

Blue beads

⑧

c. Whipstitch to bag.

Outer panel

Quilt batting

⑤

2cm

Backing

a. Sew with right sides togeher.

14cm

Attach ribbon with 2 black beads.

⑥

1.5cm

1cm

11cm

0.8cm

b Fold edges over seams and whipstitch in place.

Continued from P. 19

10. Assemble outer sole, quilt batting and backing. Quilt as shown in illustration.
11. Assemble linen facing and inner sole. Baste on outer edge of finished line. Machine stitch.
12. With right sides together, sew side seams of front and back to make a tube.
13. With right sides together, sew side seams of front and back backing fabric to make a tube.
14. Assemble (12) and (13) with wrong sides together. With right sides together, bind sole and assembled (12) and (13) with bias strip. Finish seams.

15. Sew handles and attach to top edge of bag.
16. Turn edges of backing under and whipstitch to bag.

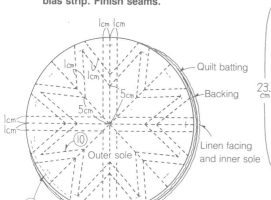

1cm 1cm

1cm

1cm

5cm

5cm

Quilt batting

Backing

1cm
1cm

⑩

Outer sole

Linen facing and inner sole

⑪

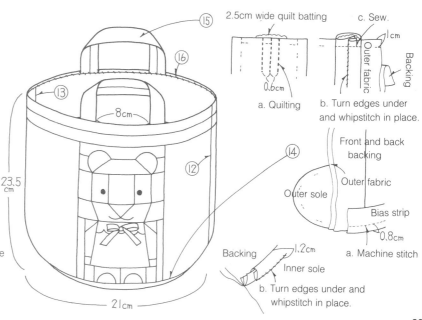

⑮

2.5cm wide quilt batting

c. Sew.

1cm

⑯

⑬

8cm

0.6cm

a. Quilting

Outer fabric

Backing

b. Turn edges under and whipstitch in place.

23.5cm

⑫

⑭

Front and back backing

Outer fabric

Outer sole

Bias strip

0.8cm

a. Machine stitch

Backing

1.2cm

Inner sole

b. Turn edges under and whipstitch in place.

21cm

Continued from P. 55

[Quilting Pattern]

Enlarge to indicated size.

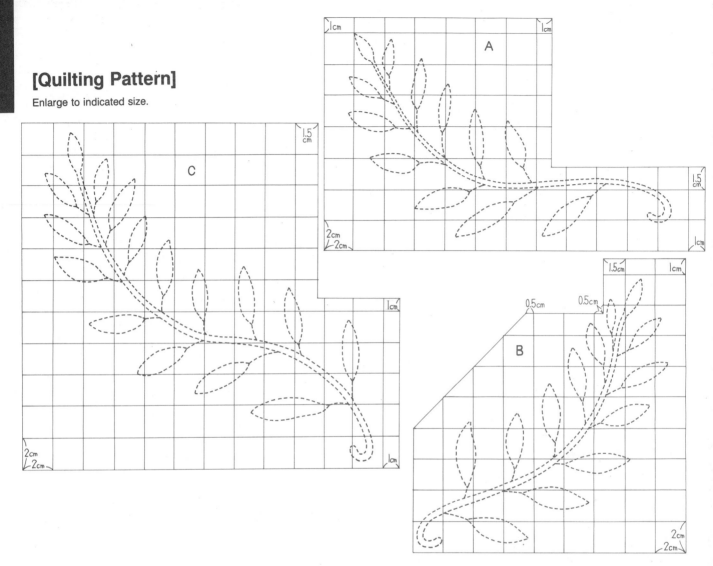

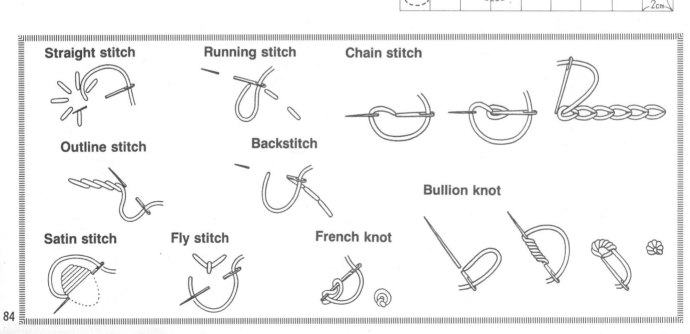

Straight stitch

Running stitch

Chain stitch

Outline stitch

Backstitch

Bullion knot

Satin stitch

Fly stitch

French knot